CLARITY, COMMUNICATION & CONNECTION

THREE CLEAR STEPS TO FUTURE-PROOF YOUR BUSINESS

LUCY RENNIE

authors
AND CO.

CONTENTS

ACCESS YOUR COMPLIMENTARY RESOURCES

To help and support you as you work your way through this book, I have created some complimentary resources, including a downloadable workbook that contains the templates, tools and activities that are mentioned throughout the different chapters, some video content and a checklist containing links to all the books, extra resources and key people that I refer to within the book.

You can access all the bonus material here: www.iamlucyrennie.com

I can't wait to see how you get on,

Lucy x

DEDICATION

I want to thank my best friend and husband, Paul Rennie, for his never-ending support and constant encouragement. There is absolutely no way I could have done any of this without you.

Thank you to our gorgeous children, Joshua and Ellia, for being so incredibly amazing. You have been my motivation to write this book, and I want to show you that you can do anything you want to do. All you have to do is decide.

And finally, thank you to all my wonderful clients for your continued support and confidence. I genuinely love working with each of you and can't wait to see what lies ahead.

Lots of love,

Lucy x

INTRODUCTION

Urgh! That dreaded sick feeling at the bottom of your tummy when you're lying awake at 2 am thinking about everything you need to do this week. You have no idea where to start, what to focus on or how you will ever get off this rollercoaster ride that is running your own business and finally feel like you're in control.

It wasn't supposed to be like this, was it? Leaving the *9 to 5* to set up by yourself was meant to bring freedom, satisfaction, and joy, not a never-ending to-do list, working all hours of the day and burnout.

From the outside looking in, becoming your own boss sounds magical! Being able to do what you love as your day job, with the added bonus of having no one telling you what to do or what you should be doing next.

Getting started, making sales, and reaching six or seven figures seemed easy and effortless, like those *'overnight success stories'* that our social media feeds are filled with day in and day out. But unfortunately, as you and I know, the reality is far from this perfect picture. Running your own business is probably one of the hardest things in the world to take on. You end up working every hour of the day, including evenings and weekends, as you try to get on top of all the plates you're spinning. The majority of your time is not spent doing the things you love doing and the reason you set out on this journey. Instead, you're juggling invoices, emails and admin and constantly worrying about where your next sale will come from and how you will cover all your expenses and pay yourself a wage this month.

Isn't it strange how suddenly everyone seems to have an opinion and be an expert? Friends and family who know best, telling you what you should or should not be spending your time and money on.

You've not become a business owner; you're a professional fire-fighter instead!

Shooting from the hip, going from one task to the next and trying to cope with the constant feeling of overwhelm is exhausting. You're beginning to feel fed up and out of control, and you're even starting to resent your business.

This is where my *Three Clear Steps to Future-Proofing your Business* comes in. I can help you take back control of your business and do what you need to do to create the success you're looking for.

I'm a huge believer in the fact that people do business with people. I believe that the key to creating a solid, successful, and sustainable business is to harness the power of your relationships and your connections and build trust and goodwill.

I want to help you to create a bank of your own personal cheerleaders who love everything you do, your products and services and want to shout about you and your business from the rooftops.

You wouldn't start putting your new wooden flooring down in your living room before you finish building the walls and painting the ceiling. And it's just the same for your business. You need to create solid foundations and get clear on what you want to achieve and whom you're going to help before you start thinking about which TikTok video you need to make next.

By taking some time out to focus on these three clear steps, I promise that you'll not only feel more in control, but you'll also be attracting more of the right kind of people to your business and, at the same time, future-proofing your brand for the months and year ahead.

So, what are my three clear steps to set you up for success?

1. **Clarity.** About who you are, why you do what you do and what you and your business stand for. Get clear on who you want to help, how you add value and why those people should buy from you.
2. **Communication.** It's all about Communication! A focus on bringing your brand to life. Telling your story in a way that engages with your audience, helps people to get to know you and your brand and builds trust and goodwill.
3. **Connection.** People buy from people. Building relationships, developing rapport, and growing and nurturing your own unique network - a bank of cheerleaders who love what you do so much that they will shout about you from the rooftops. There is no better marketing than word-of-mouth marketing, which is the key to creating a sustainable business.

I have always been curious about the ins and outs of business, looking to learn and understand the drivers to success and the common themes you need to work on to achieve your goals and objectives and get the results you are looking for.

This carried on throughout my professional career, from supporting the European teams as they designed and built together, from the different corners of Europe, the first Airbus A380, to the production line at Scania trucks and how thanks to the Japanese concept of lean manufacturing, the floor was so clean you could eat off it.

This came into play in my role as Head of Communications at ArcelorMittal Downstream, where for five years, I looked after the communication and marketing strategies for more than three hundred and fifty different steel processing and distribution sites around the world. I worked with the various leaders and helped them communicate in such a way that they could engage and motivate their people and teams and build trust and solid partnerships with their clients and other key stakeholders.

This love for people and communication is what led me to set up my own business, LR Comms, over seven years ago and where today, I have helped hundreds of small business owners and their teams to take back control, get the results they want and at the same time future-proof their businesses.

So with this in mind, I'd like you to take a few minutes to imagine how different your life would be if you could feel more in control, had a clear plan and focus, and knew you had more than enough revenue with a clear pipeline of sales.

Gone with the constant worry and sick feeling at the bottom of your tummy, instead, excited butterflies, more time to spend with your family and friends and more of that feeling of joy!

Reconnecting with the joy of doing what you love, seeing the impact that your product or service has in the world and enjoying the freedom that comes with running your own business and making your own decisions.

Just imagine how different you'd feel if you knew exactly what you stand for, if you were attracting only those 'perfect' clients and were charging what you should be charging. In other words, your pricing is just right and enables you to provide the right service and value for your clients. How different would your life be if you could sleep through the night again without worrying about how you will pay your suppliers, your team, or your mortgage?

Imagine if your days were filled with more 'buzz' moments; you know when you literally can't stop smiling, you're glowing and buzzing from the joy that comes from doing what you're good at and what you love best.

When you can step back and look at the impact you're having on your customers, your team or quite simply your family and friends. The opportunities that you've created for your loved ones thanks to your small business and your passion and determination.

The best thing about my three-step framework is that I know it works. I've seen it work, and I have seen the impact it can have on my clients' lives, their businesses and their futures.

I have worked with hundreds of business owners over the last twenty-five years, and the results speak for themselves.

Of course, I have also created my own six-figure business by following the exact process.

So, I want to make you a big promise today. A big hairy scary promise that if you come with me on this journey, if you come with me through this book and carry out all the different steps, actions, and tasks that I invite you to do, I guarantee you will change the way you live your life. You will be in a very different place for you personally and your business.

I believe that running a small business is about more than just the numbers; it's about more than selling your product or service. I believe it's about those butterflies in your tummy, those tummy flip moments when you hit your goals or you see the difference you're making in the world.

I think it takes a special kind of person to become a small business owner, and I want to do everything I can to help you achieve the success you deserve and create something extraordinary that will stand the test of time.

I want this book to become your "go-to" handbook, guide, and friend. It is not a stuffy textbook full of unpronounceable jargon, complicated formulae, or theories. Instead, it is easy to follow and full of simple-to-implement activities and exercises that will take you through the three key steps and ensure you have the solid foundations you need in your business to make it sustainable and deliver for you time after time.

Each of the three steps are broken down into different chapters that will get you thinking, asking questions, and working out the things that are important to you as a business owner.

Part 1 - Clarity

We will explore:

- What does it mean to Future-Proof your business?
- For the love of small business
- An Inside Out Approach
- Defining your brand
- Who are you here to help?

Part 2 - Communication

We will explore:

- Building trust
- Bringing your brand to life
- Telling stories
- Becoming the brand that does
- Excellent communication

Part 3 - Connection

We will explore:

- The Power of Word of Mouth
- Exploring opportunities
- The TripAdvisor Effect

Finally, the icing on the cake will be when you reach the final section and conclusion of the book, and you see that everything slots into place. It's a bit like one of those mystical adventures you might watch curled up in front of the fire with your family, like Indiana Jones or Star Wars. As each part of the puzzle falls into place, that's when the magic happens, the door opens, and the treasure is released.

Each of the three steps in the framework is of equal importance and only when they have all been given time and attention will the magic of the Ripple Effect begin.

So, are you ready? Are you ready to start and come on this adventure with me to change your business and rediscover the joy and freedom you set out to create when you decided to become a small business owner?

Exercise:

Before you get stuck in, don't forget to visit my website www. iamlucyrennie.com

And download a copy of the free downloadable workbook I have created to accompany this book and guide you through the different activities, resources and exercises.

PART 1

CLARITY

1

FUTURE-PROOF YOUR BUSINESS

Definition:

Future-proof: to make or plan something in such a way that it will not become ineffective or unsuitable for use in the future.[1]

––––––

What does Future-Proofing your business actually mean?

After working with so many business owners and their teams over the last thirty years and developing and growing my own business, I have experienced many of the highs and the lows that come from building and managing a small business.

I understand the rollercoaster ride that is running your own business.

And I get that no matter what you see on social media, regardless of how easy it can look from the outside looking in and how glamorous the entrepreneurial life may seem, the simple fact is that building a business, a successful and sustainable business, can be challenging, and it takes time.

I'm almost afraid to say it out loud, but there really is no magic pill that can transform your business or turn you into a success overnight.

For the first five years of my business, I lived with that dreaded sick and icky feeling that was always there at the bottom of my stomach as I worried about how I was going to get everything done or whether I was going to make enough sales to pay the bills at home that month.

I would worry about whether my clients were happy, asking myself if I was doing enough or if I could do more. And every time the phone rang, my tummy would flip, and I would fear the worst.

My days were a constant whirlwind, juggling clients, projects, and life. I never had enough time to do anything properly, I was always chasing my tail, and it was super hard to switch off and enjoy the rewards of running my own business. I didn't get to spend much quality time with my family, and when I did, I was constantly feeling guilty that I wasn't working; then, when I was working, I would feel guilty for not being with the kids and Paul, my husband. I even remember one Christmas Eve sitting up late after everyone was in bed and working on a Facebook ads campaign for a client that needed to be sorted and scheduled.

Although I loved what I did, communications and marketing have always been my passion; I was beginning to resent my work. It wasn't as much fun anymore; the joy had disappeared, and I was tired.

And then lockdown happened in March 2020, and everything changed. The world turned upside down, and everything slowed down. Priorities changed, people started looking for different things, and those things that had once seemed so imperative to me became obsolete.

Something clicked inside of me, and my gut instinct kicked in. I realised that people were going to need a different kind of support and that, what was, of course, a tough and trying situation could turn into an excellent opportunity for those businesses and business owners who could show up and create the value people were looking for.

I decided that the best and most certain way to succeed during the crisis would be to come from a place of integrity, trust, and simply going above and beyond. In times of uncertainty and hardship, people show their true colours and stand out from the crowd and for some reason, managing a crisis has always been my strong point.

So, I created a free Facebook community called *Communicate with Purpose* and invited small business owners from my network to join me every Thursday evening on Zoom as I shared tips and tricks on communicating effectively, exploring opportunities, how to create engaging content, and lots more. I held eighty-four Zoom workshops during the two years of lockdown, which was the catalyst to my decision to change how I worked and delivered value to my clients.

I realised that the best way for me to partner with my clients and help and support them was at a strategic level. In other words, supporting them in defining their strategy, building their roadmap and being a trusted partner and sounding board to help them achieve their goals.

With that in mind, I embarked on an *ILM Coaching and Mentoring qualification* with the brilliant Claire Bradshaw, a wonderful friend and client. This course changed my life and perspective on everything and helped me transform my business and brand into what it is today. Since then, I have been intentional about the direction I am going in, the work I take on, and the clients I work with. I am incredibly grateful for all the opportunities that have presented themselves, including writing this book. I am super excited about what the future holds as I finally understand what I am good at, helping small business owners like you to future-proof your business.

Sack loads of grit

Over the last twenty-five years, I have worked in many different businesses worldwide, watched and learned and tried things out in my own business, and helped hundreds of my own clients grow their businesses. I have come to recognise that there is no magic at play and no better way, in my opinion, to build your business other than doing the work, showing up consistently, and growing trust and goodwill.

It isn't rocket science, and you don't have to be the most talented at what you do or even be the best entrepreneur. However, it will take much hard work, determination and a lot of grit to keep going, to pick yourself up again and again and get yourself to a position where you can feel in control, be content, and fall in love with your business.

These *Three Clear Steps to Future-Proof your Business* are the key drivers that I believe will help you to build a solid business that works and feels good for you, that you can be proud of, and that people want to shout about from the rooftops.

There is no one-size-fits-all business; I want to encourage you and reassure you that the more you can embrace your individuality, vision, and way of doing things, the more successful you will be. And the more you will be able to become a magnet for your kind of people, the people who LOVE what you do, who trust you and who will keep coming back for more.

If you're at the beginning of your journey as a small business owner or already a few years in, I promise you that you can do this.

In this book, I have tried to bring together my thoughts and the ways of doing things that have worked for my clients and for me. I want to share with you the tools and resources that I've created, learned, and developed over the last few years and that have proven themselves time and time again.

There may be things you already have in place, or maybe something you did a while ago and forgot about. There may be things that you don't like the look of or have tried already, and that's ok too.

I am also continually learning, listening, and tweaking. So, I would be eternally grateful to you if you would like to get in touch, share what works for you or doesn't work so well, or maybe you have your way of approaching some of the methods or tools that you would like to share with me. I would love to hear your thoughts.

You can reach me at lucy@lrcomms.co.uk — and by the way, there's only me hiding behind there, Lucy.

It's a new world we're living in!

Times are changing. As I write this book in July 2022, we have just come out of a global pandemic, and things are very different. People want another way of life; they have different expectations and are looking for much more from their favourite brands.

Our world is changing!

Not only are we living in a VUCA world;

- Volatility
- Uncertainty
- Complexity
- Ambiguity

Here in the UK, we are also experiencing the impact of Brexit and the war in Ukraine, and it looks very likely that we are heading into a recession.

Over the last 12 months, we have seen that people are starting to re-evaluate how they want to live their lives and how they see the world of work. This change in behaviour is so substantial that it has even been given the name **The Great Resignation.**

 "New research by Ipsos in the UK finds that 47% of British workers say that in the last three months they have either thought about quitting their job (26%), looked for another job (29%), applied for another job (13%) or spoken to their employer about resigning (6%)".

IPSOS FEBRUARY 2022.

The shift is becoming so great that the emphasis is now on organisations and employers to work hard to attract the right kind of people. Businesses need to sell themselves to new employees and create strategies to ensure that they can retain and nurture their existing employees and teams.

Not only are they questioning how they want to work, whether hybrid working, home-working or other, but their expectations are also changing. Employees now want to work for organisations that mean something to them, organisations that share their values and have a clear vision and purpose.

If we add into this mix **Generation Z**, who are often less motivated by higher salaries and prefer to prioritise an improved work-life balance and quality of life, the change is dramatic.

And the same can be said for consumers.

Consumers are changing the way that they interact with brands too. They are becoming more curious, intentional, and selective as they prefer to engage with brands that have a defined purpose and that stand for something. They are interested in value-led companies that are ethical and able to show that they really care about them as customers, the planet, and the wider community.

…. consumers increasingly expect brands to "take a stand." The point is not to have a politically correct position on a broad range of topics. It is to choose the specific topics (or causes) that make sense for a brand and its consumers and to have something clear to say about those particular issues. In a transparent world, younger consumers don't distinguish between the ethics of a brand, the company that owns it, and its network of partners

and suppliers. A company's actions must match its ideals, and those ideals must permeate the entire stakeholder system.

https://www.mckinsey.com/industries/consumer-packaged-goods/our-insights/true-gen-generation-z-and-its-implications-for-companies

The **B-Corp movement** is an excellent example of this, as it encourages people to change the way that they view and interact with businesses and the way companies define success —promoting the idea that businesses should become a **"force for good"** and strive to impact and serve more than just their shareholders. Gone is the traditional role of organisations of focusing purely on making a profit and rewarding the select and privileged few.

 "Our most challenging global problems cannot be solved by governments and non-profits alone. By harnessing the power of their business, B Corps commit to positively impact all stakeholders − workers, communities, customers, and our planet."

BCORPORATION.UK

So what does this mean for you and your business?

It's time for businesses and organisations to wake up.

Most of the more prominent brands are starting to realise that they can't continue with the traditional ways of doing things anymore. They have to change the way they work, the way they behave and the way they communicate.

As a Business, you are now expected to play a more significant role in our broader society and to be intentional about how you impact people, the planet and the global economy.

It's time to become a business that does good.

This is a perfect time for businesses like yours. For people who want to create something unique, believe in what they do and want to make an impact and add value.

This is a massive opportunity for you to get it right, stand out from the crowd in the best way, and future-proof your business.

2

FOR THE LOVE OF SMALL BUSINESS

I have to talk to you about my absolute love for small business. I'm a massive believer in the fact that people do business with people. I love nothing better than seeing the magic that happens when small business owners understand the tremendous impact they can create by being themselves, telling their story and focusing on building relationships and connecting with others.

I'm on a mission to help small business owners like you benefit from the magic that happens, the incredible ripple effect that comes from growing a successful business and brand that is trusted, loved, and makes a difference.

I have worked with hundreds of business owners and entrepreneurs like you over the last twenty-plus years, as well as building and growing my own brand since 2015, so I know how challenging it can be. I recognise how much energy it takes and the enormous determination, grit, and hard work it needs to get on and hold on to the rollercoaster ride that is running and growing your own business.

I also recognise how difficult it can be to stay on track, stay in your own lane and create a business that really does work for you. There is so much pressure out there to grow, scale, and do things in a certain way. And then it seems like everybody you know has their own opinion and helpful advice that, of course, they need to share with you, to help you to "get it right"!

I'm writing this book, which is the scariest thing I have ever done in my life, because I genuinely want to help you, to share with you some of the things that have allowed me to grow my own six-figure business over the last seven years and how I have helped hundreds of my clients to build and develop their businesses. Some of them have been just starting out and I have seen them celebrate making their first sales; some have doubled in size from £2.5 million to just over £ 5 million, and many in between. I also want to share with you my learnings from over thirty years working in marketing and communications in huge global companies worldwide, but just as much from the local village pharmacy where I worked for years after school and on the weekends.

All these different experiences have taught me, and I firmly believe today, that business is all about people and that what matters is building a company that works for you, feels good and ultimately makes a difference. It doesn't have to be about scaling or growing in size; it is about creating an experience, doing what you do best and adding value to your clients and key stakeholders.

I want to help you create a business that you can be proud of, a sustainable business, and a business that you love. This book is my way of reaching out to you to share what I have learned, provide you with some tools, ideas, and resources and hopefully encourage and inspire you to recognise that you are doing a good job and to have the confidence to keep going and future-proof your business.

The Joy Factor

Since I launched my business and brand seven years ago, it has been a constant learning curve, and it has not always been an easy ride!

From day one, I have worked with numerous business advisors, coaches, growth hubs, entrepreneurial hubs, networking groups, masterminds, strategic boards, training workshops and programmes. Not to mention all the business development books and podcasts I have consumed along the way. You name it, I have probably been a part of it or had experience of it. I have always been involved in some form of business development programme. I believe it's essential to surround yourself with the right people who will help you grow, put yourself out of your comfort zone and inspire and encourage you at the same time. Even in 2022, as I write this book, I am a member of the brilliant Lisa Johnson's mastermind *Destination Inspiration*.

I think it's incredible just how much support is available for small businesses, entrepreneurs, and start-ups. The number of free resources you can access to help you grow and develop comes in many shapes and forms.

NB: Check out the link on my website and the bonus chapters to this book where I signpost you to my favourite books, podcasts, resources, and websites.

www.iamlucyrennie.com

However, I want to talk about the fact that there seems to be so much emphasis on the need to grow, scale and make lots of money as quickly as possible. It appears that the bigger you can be, the quicker you can grow, and the more you can do at once are the criteria for success and the idea that you need to hustle and work every hour of every day to get there.

Ever since the first entrepreneurial hub I joined back in 2017, I was encouraged to scale, look for investment and create huge goals for myself that frankly were not realistic, created a lot of stress and propelled me into a world of bullsh*t.

And I wasn't alone. It was a standing joke with Dan, one of my fellow business owners in the hub, that whenever anyone asked you how things were going, you'd reply - "amazing, yeah, really well, thanks," even though in reality, you were desperately trying to make ends meet, eating baked beans for tea every night and wondering how on earth you got there.

I have also worked with certain coaches who push you to become a constant machine, to work 24 / 7 and set targets that are not attainable without working yourself to the ground.

And I have witnessed the stress, burnout and general unhappiness that set in amongst my friends and other members of the groups as they worked every hour and never switched off.

Social media and the 'entrepreneurial' hype go a long way in supporting this ethos too, with all the reels, videos and memes glorifying the hustle, the non-stop work ethic, and the idea that it's a good thing to be in that constant stressed state.

The result of all this pressure to perform, to deliver and to be 'on it' constantly is that not only do you risk making yourself seriously ill, but you also begin to fall out of love with your business, with your baby, and I know that for me when that happens, it's the beginning of the end.

Over the last few years, I have realised that it does not have to be that way. There are no rules on how you should run your own business, and no one can define what success looks like other than yourself.

Who says that bigger is better, that you need to make millions or that you need to have a huge team to succeed?

What if we looked at things differently and started from a place of 'joy'?

I believe that as a business owner finding and focusing on joy is the key to creating a successful business for the future.

Most people begin a business because they are looking for a different life; maybe they are leaving a job behind, a demanding boss or they want to spend more time doing the things they love.

Whatever your reason, building your own business is not an easy ride, so being able to tap into the things that motivate you, that you enjoy and that bring you joy are super important.

You will have your way of defining what success looks like for you. I'm on a mission to help small business owners like you create a business that works for you, feels good and that you love. I believe that if you want to build something sustainable and that keeps on giving, if you want to future-proof your business, then you need to find and nurture the things that bring you joy.

You need to be in it for the long game.

There are a few things that I want to share with you here that are important to me. Firstly, I want to bust the myth that says you can build a successful business overnight. Of course, there are a few exceptions, but 99.9% of all businesses have been working at it for months, years, decades, and in some cases more than that before they can experience the kind of success they are looking for. Even those who appear to have suddenly become famous through a post or video going viral have, in reality, been working hard at it for years.

I would also like to call out the numerous unethical coaches, mentors, and business "gurus" that we see predominantly in the online space who are continually selling and promoting the notion that you can create a six-figure launch without growing an audience or having an established brand.

This is all nonsense and is wrong on many levels.

For me, though, I want to talk to you about needing to be in it for the long game because I genuinely believe that the most effective and sustainable way to grow your small business is by developing goodwill, trust, and word-of-mouth referrals. And to do that, it is going to take time, patience, and consistency.

In this book, I will take you through my three clear steps: Clarity, Communication and Connection, which I believe are the solid foundations that will allow you to engage with your people, add value and grow your bank of goodwill and reputation. There are no quick fixes or cheap tactics to get there faster. If you genuinely want to build and future-proof a fantastic business, then I believe you need to accept and embrace the fact that you are in it for the long game.

Value

This is the essence of everything I know about small business. If you come from a real, honest, and integral place of value, then I promise you'll make things happen. I have heard many discussions over the years about how much value you should add, whether you should create free content, how much you should help people and whether or not you should go the extra mile.

I would like to lay my cards down on the table right now and let you know that I believe you should give as much value as possible and then give more. I have seen the impact that coming from a genuine place of wanting to help people can have on your business, and I promise that it will be worth your while every single time.

Going above and beyond for your clients and your people will never be a waste of time. But you need to come from a place of absolute integrity and sincerity. If you are doing something with a view to gaining a reward or getting something in return, if you are showing up and you are out of integrity and not being your authentic self, then people will know immediately, and the effect will be the opposite.

I know I said that there is no magic pill or bullet to growing your business, that you must put the work in and show up consistently. And although I wholeheartedly agree with this, I also believe that you can create your own magic, which comes from adding value time after time.

Energy

Have you ever witnessed the energy that certain people bring with them? You can see it sometimes as they walk in and light up a room, the whole vibe changes.

It can be pretty hard to put your finger on what is at play exactly, but you know that the person has a certain kind of energy about them, and they can make you feel a particular way.

We don't talk about these kinds of things much, and you don't read about them in the business growth manuals. Still, I believe that the energy that surrounds your business and your brand is key and has the power to make people feel something special.

The energy you bring when you show up in your business is just as important. Be intentional about how you are, how you inter-act, and how you want people to feel when they engage with you and your brand.

———

Exercise:

Note down your thoughts on these questions.

- What do people feel when you enter the room?
- What would you like them to feel?
- What action can you take to ensure you show up with the right energy every time?

———

3

AN INSIDE OUT APPROACH TO YOUR BRAND

What is the Inside Out approach?

At the heart of any successful and sustainable brand, you will find a strong vision, mission and purpose, and clearly identified values that represent what you do, how you do it and why you do it. These are the foundations that prepare your business and brand for success. Once you have defined and embedded these elements within your business, you will see that they begin to influence everything that happens. Whether that is the goals you create, the new products or services you develop, the way you communicate, the people you attract, the people you work with, and even the way you spend your time and energy. Everything will be driven from these foundations, so it's imperative to make sure you get them right.

As the business owner and the founder of your brand, you are responsible for setting the tone, for painting the picture of your business and how you want it to come to life and make an impact. You are responsible for how your brand evolves, the culture created and how things get done, which means that everything has to start with you. You have to lead by example in everything you do.

I believe that if you are truly going to create something unique and sustainable, then it needs to come from the inside. I believe that it starts with you; it comes from what makes you tick, from what's inside of you and what is important to you. It grows from your dreams, your passion, and your beliefs.

It's an Inside Out approach.

Creating a strong vision

It's essential to take some time to understand, identify and capture the vision for your brand. Define and communicate what you want your brand to look and feel like and where you want your brand to be in the future and the impact that you want to have on the world.

This is the bigger picture thinking, the part that can seem a bit *woo* to some, but it's also the part that is incredibly important to get right.

It sounds obvious when you think about it. But how can you know which road you need to take or which direction you need to go in if you don't know where you want to go or where you want to be?

Can you imagine getting into your car one Saturday afternoon with all your family and just setting off to the airport to go on holiday? Not making any plans, not booking any flights and not preparing for any accommodation, meals or activities. What would happen?

OK, so you might have a bit of fun at first, I agree that there's nothing like a bit of spontaneity, but it wouldn't last long. You'd soon get stuck! You wouldn't get far without a destination, ticket, and itinerary!

The point is that without a vision and a strategy, it's not sustainable.

I believe that if you want to build a business that works for you and feels good, then you need to have an idea in your mind of what that looks like. You need to identify what that bigger picture is to create the strategy and roadmap to help you to get there.

I have worked with so many business owners who don't have a vision or a plan, or sometimes they did have one in the beginning, but it kind of got lost on the way.

You know what it's like when you start your business; it can take so much energy to get it up and running. You begin to make some sales, and things seem to be moving in the right direction, and then you get so busy that you forget why you started in the first place and what you were trying to achieve.

It's so easy to become so caught up in the day-to-day running of their business, the firefighting, and the spinning of all the plates that you lose sight of what you should be focusing on, so you end up treading water and, in some cases, drowning.

Honestly, I think this has almost become the norm for many small business owners. Having a plan and a strategy seems to become a *must* only when they need to borrow money from the bank or are looking for investment. Otherwise, it has almost become a bit of a joke; who needs a plan?

This is how that icky feeling starts; you're so caught up in the doing that you forget where you are going and no longer feel in control.

You start to lose sight of the joy. You lose sight of the things you enjoy, and you get frustrated, or you start to resent what you're doing, and you begin to fall out of love with your business.

That's not going to be you though. Starting today, you are going to get crystal clear on your vision for your brand and where you want to be. I'm going to help you get to grips with what it looks like and feels like. And understand what it means for you and your business.

And the best way to do this is to start with the end in mind.

A little bit of my story

During lockdown in the global Coronavirus pandemic in 2020, I realised I needed to take some time to reflect and think about what I wanted for my business and what I wanted to do with my life.

I too had lost sight of why I had started on this journey. I realised that I had found myself stuck on the constant hamster wheel looking after lots of clients and a team and not being able to enjoy my work, life, family, or kids, which was ultimately why I was doing it.

I put my out-of-office on for a few days and took some time out to focus on myself and work out what I wanted. Through journaling, digging deep and really looking hard at what was working for me, what was not working and then thinking about the things that made me tick, that made me happy and gave me tummy flips. I was able to identify and get clear on what was important for me and start to build a vision, to paint a picture of the life I wanted to create and of where I wanted my business to be.

I decided to pivot and move from an agency model to focus on providing more strategic support, coaching, and mentoring for my clients and other small business owners and their teams. I realised that I wanted to be able to reach more people and help and support more business owners like you, to build businesses you love and make a difference. And to do that, I needed to find some room to breathe, to be able to create the tools and resources and bring to life the programmes and communities that I had in mind. I needed to make some significant changes in the way I did things and the way I worked.

Fast forward two years pretty much to the day, 7th June 2022, and I am sitting in a cottage by the sea in Anglesey writing this book, bringing my vision to life and feeling content.

Getting under the skin of your vision.

My vision is to help small business owners like you build a successful and sustainable business that keeps on giving. I want to help you to create a business that works for you and feels good. I want you to build a business that you love.

If we can take this one step further and look at the wider environment, it goes further. I passionately believe in small business as a driver for the good of our economy, society, and future generations.

I think that small businesses have the power and the opportunity to create great things in the world, to make a positive impact on people, on our planet and in the way we do things. So, if I can play even just a small role in supporting, encouraging, and inspiring people like you to grow and future-proof a successful business, then I know that the impact I can have will be significant.

As you know, in today's new world, Generation Z are already changing how we do things. What they are looking for from businesses and organisations is completely different from what our parents' or grandparents' generation were looking for.

They want to see business playing its part in the world. They want to see businesses creating real societal impact; they want to work and buy from businesses that have a purpose, are doing 'the right thing' and are in line with their values. Businesses who stand up for what they believe.

So, for me, in my work, if I can help you as a small business owner to embrace your vision and your purpose and to hone on in on why you do what you do, then the potential impact of my work is massive.

———

Exercise: – Visualisation

A great way to help you work out your vision and where it is that you want to be is to carry out this short visualisation task.

Find a quiet place, get yourself a nice warm drink, a pen, and a piece of paper.

I want you to sit down and get comfortable, shut your eyes and then imagine that it's New Year's Eve in one year, two years, three years, four years or even ten years from now. You decide how far into the future you want to go and where you want to focus your energy.

I want you to imagine that it is early evening on New Year's Eve, and you are with the person (s) you want to be with, and of course, you've got a glass of something celebratory in your hand.

I want you to create a picture in your mind of where you are, and who you're with and then begin to imagine how you're feeling.

You are exactly where you want to be. You have achieved everything you set out to achieve and are feeling exactly how you want to feel.

Take a few minutes to settle into that moment and picture yourself there.

Then very slowly, start to look around you; what are you doing? Where are you? What are you wearing? Who are you with? What does your business look like? How has it changed? And importantly, how are you feeling?

I want you to imagine yourself sitting down and reflecting over the last year, the last two or three years or the last five or ten years, depending on how far into the future you decided to go.

Start to visualise and see all the things you have achieved, what you have created, the challenges you have overcome and the key actions you have taken. Be as detailed as you can be, and notice anything that jumps out at you or catches your attention.

Keep going, working back through your actions until you arrive right back to where you are today. I want you to imagine how pleased and thrilled you are that you've managed to create the life you were looking for.

You realise that you have managed to build the business that you wanted to create.

Set a timer on your phone for five minutes, and then keep your eyes shut; just allow yourself to feel, experience and reflect.

Then, open your eyes, take your paper and pen, and write yourself a letter.

Imagine that it's you in the future, in your mind, writing to you now and describing everything you have just visualised.

All the success, all those feelings, describe to yourself exactly where you are, what you are doing, what it feels like and then give yourself any advice, tell yourself anything you think you need to hear to get to where you want to be. How can you make it easier for yourself?

And if there are three things you want yourself to think about to focus on, to remember, to help you keep going when things get tiring or frustrating or challenging, write them down.

Then, sign the letter with love and pop it in an envelope.

How did that feel?

This exercise is brilliant in helping you to identify what it is that you are looking for. What that vision is, where you want to be for both parts of you, in your personal life, and your business.

Please keep this letter with you to draw on when you need to keep focused when you are working on your strategy and your roadmap, and of course, at those times when things get a bit tricky or challenging, and you need to remind yourself of why you are doing all this.

Once you've done it, I would love for you to get in touch and tell me how you got on. Let me know and if you are up for it, share that dream and that vision with me so that I can share with you in your vision. Send it to me at lucy@lrcomms.co.uk

––––––

Your mission

Now that you know where you want to be, you can think about what that means for your brand and the people you want to help.

Your mission is the roadmap that outlines what your brand does and how it adds value to the people you help. It sets out the actions you need to take and how you do things that move you forward towards achieving your vision.

Your mission is there to demonstrate why you and your brand are the right choice to help your customers. Getting clear on what you do and how you help enables you as a business to focus on what is important and at the same time, it allows your clients and customers to understand how you can help them and why they should trust you to deliver.

––––––

Exercise: - Your mission statement

Take some time to perfect your brand's mission statement, and keep in mind these five tips:

1. Start with you and your vision. What is the impact you want to make?
2. Keep your customers' needs and expectations in mind. What are they looking for? What's important to them?
3. Make sure it is realistic and believable. Don't sell rainbows or promises you can't keep.
4. Make sure it is easy to understand and memorable for you, your team and your customers.
5. Keep it short, simple and concise.

———

Defining your Purpose.

Purpose: *the reason for which something is done or created or for which something exists.* [1]

Your purpose is the thing that ties everything all together, brings it all to life and moves everything forward. It's the raison d'être for your business, your brand and you.

It's what makes you get up in the morning. It's what drives you and keeps you going when the s*** hits the fan, or you get tired and feel like you want to throw the towel in.

Your purpose is why you do what you do, which comes from a much deeper place that feeds off your values, beliefs and inner-most desires.

It comes with emotion and feelings and is the driver behind your choices, the work you do and the difference you want to make.

What is it that you are here to do? What is the bigger reason behind all that you do?

This can sound a bit woo, and a bit weird, and I know there are many buzzwords floating around and a lot of fluffiness around finding your purpose and getting clear on your why.

However, I do believe that to be an entrepreneur and a business owner, you need to have identified your purpose; you need to be able to focus on why you are on this journey and what makes you feel fulfilled, satisfied, and fired up.

It might take a little bit of time to unpick it and explore it, but it's important to identify the root and core of it, as this will be the catalyst for everything you do and how you drive your business. It will become the basis for why people will or won't engage and connect with you and your brand. Of why they should trust you, work with you and believe in you.

As Simon Sinek said, "People don't buy what you do; they buy why you do it and what you do simply proves what you believe."

How to identify your purpose.

One of the ways we can do this is to start to ask yourself some simple questions:

- What is it that gets you up in the morning?
- What drives you to do the things you do each day?

I want you to think about those moments when you feel *"on top of this world"*. When you know that you are buzzing and you're feeling good. When maybe something is happening, or something has happened where you have had a great result, or you have been working with a fantastic client or created a new and exciting product. Whatever that might be, think about those times and how they make you feel.

Usually, you get a funny sensation in your tummy as if it is full of butterflies doing loop the loops!

Think about what it is that you're doing when you feel those tummy flips, and you will start to identify the link between that feeling and what you are doing, and very often, the thing that drives those flips is very much linked to your purpose.

My purpose is to combine my two great passions: People and Small Business.

I love working with people, particularly business owners, entrepreneurs, and people who have a vision, and I love everything to do with small business. I believe that small business can greatly impact the world we live in.

When I combine my two passions, I can help people like you tap into why you do what you do, get excited about your business, and achieve the results you desire.

I want to inspire you and encourage you to build a business you love, to create a successful and sustainable business, one that makes a difference. That is when I get my tummy flips, I get excited, and that's when I know I am doing what I am here to do, my purpose.

———

Exercise: Ted Talk

I highly recommend you take ten minutes to watch the infamous *Ted Talk* by the fabulous Simon Sinek –

https://www.ted.com/talks/simon_sinek_how_great_leaders_inspire_action?language=en

Take some time to capture your thoughts about your purpose here. Can you create your own Golden Circle for your Vision, Mission and Purpose?

What do you stand for? And why should we care?

Everything you do as you build your business and brand should be geared towards showing up in a way that is aligned with you, your vision, mission, purpose, and your values.

If you want to attract more of your kind of people to your business, then you need to be super clear on all the above so that you can communicate effectively and in such a way that you resonate and connect with your perfect clients. You want to encourage them and inspire them and create enough curiosity within them to want to engage with you and your brand.

Today's world is a very noisy place, and everyone is busy. Therefore, you must find a way for your brand to stand out from the crowd and break through all the noise. Getting super clear on what you stand for is key.

Remember we talked about it being a long game?

You have to go deeper as you work to build your brand, grow your reputation, and create trust and goodwill. You must give your audience reasons why they should want to connect with you, why they should want to buy from you, why they should engage with you and why they should trust you.

And one of the best and most powerful ways of doing this is to stand up for what you believe. One of the best ways to stand out from the crowd is to be recognised for what you stand for, what is important to you and what you care about.

It is becoming even more relevant today in this post-pandemic world where people's priorities are changing. People are re-evaluating what is important to them. People are much more concerned about the broader impact businesses have on the world, society and the planet. And they are becoming more influenced by what lies underneath the surface of a brand, what is at the heart of a brand.

66 *"64% of those surveyed said of the generation Z are prepared to pay more for a product or service that is sustainable aligned."*[2]

66 *"Two in five say that they have rejected a job because it has not been aligned with their values."*[3]

We are moving into a society where consumers will be much more demanding towards businesses and brands and expect that they do more towards helping the climate, towards supporting mental health issues, towards more civic engagement and those bigger and wider issues in general.

In other words, people want their brands to stand for something, they want their brands to mean something, and they want to see that businesses are taking part and creating a more positive impact in the world.

Exercise: - What are your values?

This is a great exercise I do with my clients as we look to get under the skin of their business to identify their core values. The whole point of this is to do it without overthinking it and capturing the first thoughts that come into your head, as they are often the truest.

Find the values table in the workbook.

Find a pen and a stopwatch and set the time to three minutes.

I want you to fill in the first column of the table in your workbook as quickly as possible and without overthinking. I want you to write down the five most important values to you as a person and business owner.
Now, the pressure is off, and you can take all the time you need.

In the second column, I want you to describe what that particular value means to you. Maybe you could give an example of what you mean by that?

And finally, in the third column, I'd like you to answer the question - So what!? Why should anyone care?
So, for example, if you put down 'honesty' as one of your values, you might describe honesty as being truthful and frank in the way you behave and communicate. For your clients, that might mean they can trust you to be honest with them, to be realistic and perhaps they can count on you to tell them things that they may not like to hear but probably need to hear.

These are the foundations of your business and the key to how your organisation will function. Everything you do should have your vision, purpose and values in mind, whether creating new products or services, recruiting new people, or saying yes or no to new partnerships. Bringing it back to what is at the core of your business will enable you to stay on track, keep focused and work in integrity with your brand.

Today's world is a busy place. Therefore, you must find a way for your brand to stand out from the crowd and break through all the noise.

If you can communicate and act from the inside out, from a place of value and purpose, and walk the talk, then you will be able to attract and retain the right kind of people, people who resonate with you and your brand and what you stand for, whether that is to join your team, as customers or to partner with you.

You will be able to build a solid reputation based on what you do and what you stand for, which is ultimately the key to thriving in this new world.

NB: If you already have a trusted team or are in a partnership, I recommend that you look at the exercises in this chapter together and think about these things in parallel, for you individually and then how you come together to make up your brand.

4

DEFINING YOUR BRAND

What is a brand?

Your brand is what distinguishes your business from another.

It is how you present your business to the world. It makes your business unique, enabling it to stand out from the crowd and attract the right kind of people, opportunities, and adventures!

Taking time out to get clear about what makes your brand special, what's important and what you have to offer is vital in growing your presence, increasing your visibility, and developing your brand.

What is reputation, and why is it important?

Your reputation is what other people think or say about you and your brand behind your back or when you are not in the room.

Ultimately you have no control over this. You cannot make people think a certain way, and you cannot make them say what you want them to say about you and your business.

Nevertheless, in today's world, your reputation as a business owner, a leader and a brand is incredibly important. It has the power to potentially make or break your business.

 "It takes twenty years to build a reputation and five minutes to ruin it. If you think about that, you'll do things differently."

> *WARREN BUFFETT*

But even if you cannot control what people think of you, that doesn't mean you cannot be intentional and strategic about it. And that's what I want you to think about here.

I'd like to invite you to be intentional about building your reputation. One that reflects your brand, your values, the real added value you deliver, and the experience you create for your customers and key stakeholders. I want you to intentionally build a reputation that works to reinforce everything you do, drives the right people to you and helps to build goodwill and trust.

The best way to start is with the end in mind. I would like you to take some time to think about what you'd like your reputation to be. In other words, what do you want people to say about you and your brand, and how do you want to be perceived?

───

Exercise: The fly on the wall.

A great exercise that I work through with my clients and one you can try is to imagine that you are a fly on the wall.

Imagine you are in a pub or an airport lounge or wherever your ideal clients hang out, and because you are a 'fly on the wall', you can see them all sitting around, talking about you and your business, and you can hear what they are saying.

Using the template in the downloadable workbook from my website, you will find a space to note down your thoughts and ideas.

Take some time to answer these fundamental questions and create a list of at least five things.

- ***What would you LIKE people to say about you and your business and why?*** *For example, you might want them to say something about the excellent quality products, or maybe you want them to say, "I love working with Lucy; she cares about me and my business, and I know she's got my back" or "it was such an excellent and amazing experience, I can't wait to do it again, and I highly recommend."*
- **Now think about why each of those is important. What is it about what you have noted down that makes you happy? Why do you want them to say that specific thing?** This is a great way to gain insight into you, your values and your vision. Where you want to be and how you want to be seen. It's a great way to understand yourself a bit more and recognise what is important to you. Make some notes and think about what's coming out for you.

- ***What would you NOT want them to say? What would be the worst thing ever?*** *The thing that would make you turn in your grave that would just be the end of the world for you. What would that be?* And again, think about why that's important and why that matters. Ask yourself why you have chosen that specific thing, how that fits into your vision and purpose, and how you want to grow the business.

———

Even though you know you cannot control what people think and say about you and your brand, you can do everything you can to help them.

In other words, if you want them to talk about how your products or services are of such high quality or you want them to feel that you care, that you've got their back, and you want them to have a fantastic experience. The only way you will get them to say those things about your brand, think those things, and believe those things is for your brand to be and deliver on those things.

In other words, you need to *'walk the talk'*.

I always think this sounds quite serious, a bit scary and full on.

But, it makes sense that if you're building a brilliant business, a business that you love, that works and does great things. If you're building on your purpose, on your vision, on your values, then this should be easy and simple, don't you think?

In other words, if you're doing what you say you're going to do, to the best of your knowledge, skill and experience, and you do care about doing a good job and coming from a place of integrity and adding value, then it should be a simple process.

As you build up your brand over time, it might not be a quick process, but we know you have to be in it for the long game.

And one of the things I love about working on your brand reputation is that you can make it tangible. It is something that you can measure and track and see evolve through customer feedback, surveys, monitoring reviews and, of course returning customers and lifetime value.

There are all sorts of different ways you can track what people are saying about you and your business, which will help to feed into measuring the level of trust and goodwill that you are creating in your business which are the critical drivers to future-proofing.

Becoming the 'go-to' brand or person for what you do.

Ultimately your goal should be to create a brand and reputation that means you can become the 'go-to' person and brand for your product or service. You want to become so good at what you do and so well known for it that people come to associate you and your brand with what you do, and they recommend and refer you to their friends and colleagues.

What is it that you want to be known for?

———

Exercise:

Imagine your clients are talking to people who have never heard of you before. They are having a chat in the pub or at baby group or wherever they hang out, and one of their friends or colleagues is saying I need this, or I have got this problem, and I need a solution, or I've had this challenge, and I need someone who can help me with it.

What would you like people to say about your brand, how should they describe you, and what do you want to be known for?

Example:

 "Oh, you should speak to Lucy Rennie because she's the go-to person for helping you build and future-proof your small business; she can help you to develop a strategy and roadmap that works for you."

How can you expect other people to be clear about this if you are not? By getting clear and focused on what you want your brand to be known for, you can then be strategic and intentional in how you communicate and grow your brand and reputation.

Write down the answers to these questions.

- What are you the 'go-to' person or brand for?
- How would you like to be introduced at a party?

Finish this sentence.... *Hi, I'd like you to meet (insert your name). (Your name) is an expert in (insert) and works with (insert your ideal client) to (insert how you help – the problem you solve).*

I know it seems tedious thinking about this and doing these exercises, but I urge you to take some time to think through them and try them out properly.

Write some ideas down and then test them. Say them out loud, try them out at meetings or dinner parties and introduce yourself and your brand. See how it feels for you and see how it fits.

How does your tummy feel when you say them out loud? Do they feel right?

By getting intentional, you can influence what people say about you. You can give your audience the words they need to describe you, introduce you and your brand, talk about you, and spread the word about you to others.

If you don't get intentional, you will find that they'll choose their own words, make up their own description for your brand, and introduce you in their own way, which may or may not be how you would like them to.

Becoming the 'go-to' expert, the 'go-to' person in your industry, the 'go-to' brand in your field, in your market is where the power lies. It is the essence of building your brand, of word-of-mouth marketing and future-proofing your business.

We want your name and brand to be on the tips of everybody's tongues, ready to reach all those people who need your support and help, your products and services. This is the first step to igniting the ripple effect and achieving consistent word-of-mouth marketing.

What is it that makes you special?

Who are you to build a business doing what you're doing?

We are going to talk about your USP or your 'unique selling proposition' later in this chapter, but one thing I want to get across to you early on as we are thinking about future-proofing your business and about building your brand is about creating a business that works and feels good for you.

It's important to understand that the *one thing* that makes your business unique, the *one thing* that makes you stand out from the crowd and the *one thing* that you have complete control over is you.

This is important for two main reasons. The first reason is, on a personal level, for you as a business owner. At some point in time, when you are on that rollercoaster ride, fighting fires and maybe having a bit of a bad day, you'll find yourself doubting yourself or questioning yourself and thinking....

"Who am I to be doing this?"

This is where I want you to come back and remind yourself of what it is that makes you special and be able to give yourself the confidence boost that you deserve.

The second reason is that getting clear on who you are, what your DNA is, what your Lego bricks are and what makes you who you are, enables you to distinguish yourself and your brand and differentiate yourself from your competition.

I promise you that nobody else on this planet is quite like you, with the same DNA, building blocks, experience, and expertise as you.

Nobody else has your unique perspective on things and looks at the world or sees things the way you do.

This is what makes you special and what makes you unique, which in turn makes your business unique and stand out from everything else.

It is incredibly exciting, and it fires me up just thinking about the endless opportunities available to you and your brand simply because you are your unique self.

I invite you to spend some time on this and to capture as much as possible in the next exercise because this is going to feed into the second part of the Future-Proof framework, which is all about how you communicate your story, your value, and your experience to attract your kind of people and build that trust and goodwill.

The more we can tap into your uniqueness, the easier it will be to identify and attract clients that fit with your brand, that get you, that want to work with you, and ultimately you know you perform at your best with.

———

Exercise: - The CV of your life.

It's time to write your CV, but not just any CV. I want you to map out the CV of your life.

Take some time to reflect and think back, right back to the beginning, as far back as you can remember.

You can do this in different ways. You might want to make a mind map and scribble everything down. You might want to draw a big timeline and plot different things on that timeline, or you might want to write it as a story or as a letter. You might even want to draw a picture. It's entirely up to you.

But what I'd like you to do is to think back as far back as you can, think about all the things you have achieved in your life. Identify all the success stories, all those significant milestones, all those big things that you've done, you've experienced, that you've seen throughout your lifetime.

I want you to think about the little things too. So yes, it might be big things like learning how to play the trumpet, going on a work experience holiday to France, learning to speak Italian, qualifying as an English teacher, or learning to drive.

It could be getting your first client; it might be moving to a different country, or it might be getting married. It might be winning an award for something, completing a project, learning how to cook, or having your first child. Whatever they might be, I want you to note them down, think about them, and remember them.

Remember how you felt about them. Maybe there were failures, or maybe there were things that didn't quite go to plan but that you learned from. Think about and capture all the things that have made you who you are today. All the things that have contributed to the person you are today, perhaps more determined, more resilient, and more motivated than ever.

No detail is too small. Remember, you don't have to share this with anybody. But this is for you to take stock and witness the enormity of everything you have already achieved in your life.

Now I want you to sit back and smile as you celebrate everything that makes you special.

As you worked through this, you will have noticed that there have been some key sections or chapters that make up your life until now, and you will have seen that there were times when you had to level up, where a shift has had to happen. It is fascinating to notice those things and capture them as it will help you in the future as you are confronted with new challenges and you need to level up once more. Reflecting and looking back at how you overcame the last hurdles will give you the strength to carry on and get over the next ones.

When one of my mentors, Neil Simpson, asked me to do this for the first time in 2016, it was eye-opening. I was trying to grow my business and build my brand, but I was also suffering from incredibly paralysing imposter syndrome, making me question everything I was doing. *Was I good enough? Could I offer help? Who did I think I was? Could I really deliver on what I was offering?*

Completing this exercise and going back through my life, reliving some of the experiences I've had so far, helped me recognise the experience and expertise I have.

I had some big *'A-ha' moments!*

For example, I spent years working with some of the senior health and safety teams in the biggest mining and steel company around the world to create and nurture a zero-accident culture. I organised and delivered workshops for senior leaders worldwide to help them understand why engaging with their employees is crucial, giving them a voice and creating an open and transparent culture. I won an award for my 'Having your Say' initiative that made it possible for over 15,000 employees to have their say and be a part of a huge culture change.

I had forgotten about these experiences. I had kind of dismissed them and put them to the back of my mind. Revisiting them helped me to see that I was worthy of this, that I can do this, that I do have value to offer, and that helped me build up my confidence. First of all, inside me, to feel more capable, and secondly, it gave me a bank of stories to tell and gave me a narrative to be able to share with clients or my audience, which would help them to resonate with me, allow them to see that I am whom I say I am, that I have done the things I say I have, I have the experience and ultimately that I can help them with their challenges and finding solutions to their problems.

So, I recommend you take this time to revisit your journey, get under your own skin and see what comes up for you.

And don't forget to keep coming back and adding your new achievements and learnings to your CV.

Bonus suggestion: - Keep a bank of testimonials, recognition, cards and the emails you get from people thanking you for your support, describing the results that you help them to get or the way you have helped them to feel good.

Now, when you need that little boost, you can immerse yourself in all the excellent and positive feedback. It is also the best medicine when you need to remember why you are doing what you're doing and why you're the right person for the job, the expert and 'go-to' person your client needs.

Are you working in your Zone of Genius?

What if I tell you that I hate excel spreadsheets?

In fact, I hate Excel so much that if you asked me to create a pivot table with data and graphs, I would undoubtedly tear my hair out for days, trying to get my head around what I needed to do, and I would hate every second of it!

However, if you ask me to go into a room full of business owners like you and talk to them about why they do what they do and help them to get under the skin of their vision and their purpose and talk about their business, I would love and relish every second of it!

And I know I would be bloody good at it too and we would have a brilliant time. I know that the room would be buzzing, and each participant would get the results and impact they were looking for.

So, what does that mean? What is that all about? Why do some things seem easy and not like hard work, and other things can feel so challenging, complicated, and tedious?

How about those times when you are so absorbed by what you are doing, you are enjoying yourself, and if you are quite honest, it can feel too easy?

How many times have you questioned whether you have done something right, if you have done enough or done it in the right way, simply because you found it so easy and a joy to do?

What if I said to you that the reason why you find it so easy and so enjoyable is that it is in your *Zone of Genius?*

It is what you are here to do. It is what you are good at; it is your talent, your area of expertise, and so, of course if it feels easy, it's because it is easy for you. It is your *Zone of Genius.*

So why do we beat ourselves up about it, and why do we feel so uncomfortable about doing such an excellent job in something that comes so naturally to us? It doesn't make sense, does it?

Unfortunately, nobody tells us about our Zone of Genius, and they do not teach you about it at school. So, most people feel rubbish about those things, feeling as if they are not doing enough and sometimes shying away from the things they are naturally good at.

When in fact, what you should be doing is focusing on understanding what IS in your zone of genius and then doing everything in your power to make sure that you can spend as much time as possible within that zone, doing what you love and ultimately what you are good at.

―――――

Exercise:

I would like you to take some time to explore what is in your *Zone of Genius.*

- What is it that you are doing when you feel in flow? When you're buzzing because you know you have done a great job, you love what you are doing and *woohoo,* you've had a great day?
- Have a good think about what it is that you love doing and identify it, catch it, and note it down.
- How can you bring more of this into your business, into the way you work and into how you work?

Your brand pillars

We have looked at many things in this chapter, including your vision, purpose, values and what you stand for. Now it's time to start to pull it all together and think about what it means for your customer, your broader audience, and your brand.

I want you to be intentional here and to think about what you want people to know about you and what you want your brand to be associated with.

Ideally, you will have four primary areas of focus for you and your brand, and I'm going to call these your brand pillars. Each pillar should represent a specific subject or topic that is significant to you and your business and is in line with how you want your brand to be perceived by your customers and the external world.

It's like peeling back the different layers of your brand, and each time you are allowing your audience to get a taste of you, develop a greater understanding of who you are and why you do what you do and get under the skin of your brand, helping them to see whether or not you are a good fit.

The more interesting and unique you can make these pillars, the more you will stand out from the crowd, and more people will be drawn to you and your brand.

And, of course, it is much more interesting for a journalist to tell a story about your brand or incorporate your story within a publication when you are talking about something that matters to you and society as a whole.

The first pillar is about your product or service, your core offering. At a simple level, it's basically what you do and how you do it.

For example, for me it is communications and marketing support, small business strategy and mentoring; I help business owners future-proof their business. This is what I am recognised for and the first of my brand pillars. It is the top line of my messaging.

I am the 'go-to' expert in all things communication and marketing for your business.

The second pillar is linked to your beliefs and what you stand for. In other words, why you do what you do, your purpose.

For me, it is about being a champion for small business and future generations. I believe that great small business owners have the potential to change the way the world works. I believe in a place where brands do good, create amazing value, impact the wider community through their products and services and provide brilliant places to work for their teams and key partners.

This is why I do what I do and want to help small business owners like you get it right and build a business from the inside out. This is why I have created my mentoring and apprenticeship programmes, why I'm writing this book, why I've launched my *Future-Proof your Business* podcast and why I work with local schools and charities to support young people and the next generation of entrepreneurs.

Your third pillar is about you, your background and your story.

For me, it's about my twenty-five years of experience working with businesses around the world. About the fact that I spent a third of my life living in France, speaking fluent French, and working in the steel industry.

It's about my journey and experiences as an entrepreneur, about being a mum and a wife and the ins and outs of juggling these different aspects of my life. And it's about why I have chosen to live in Whaley Bridge, in the countryside and do what I do working from home.

It's about all the extraordinary things that are unique to me and make me who I am. And these are the things that help me attract my kind of people and connect and resonate with them along the way.

The fourth and final pillar is about something you believe in.

Finally, my fourth and final pillar and one if I am honest, that I'm still working on and exploring, is all about mental health, and the resilience and grit you need as an entrepreneur. This is something that I want to become incremental to my brand, what I stand for and what I'm known for.

This is close to my heart because I have suffered from anxiety and other mental health challenges throughout my life, and I am very aware that many other entrepreneurs and small business owners suffer from this too. I want to do all I can to help and bring awareness to this.

These four key brand pillars make up the different layers of your brand and will help you to create structure and a voice, allowing your brand to come into its own space, differentiate itself from the crowd and stand up for what is important.

Please note that your pillars are not set in stone and will naturally evolve as your brand grows and develops. But for now, it is time to be brave and bold and stand up for what you believe in.

––––––

Exercise:- Defining your pillars

There are no right or wrong answers to this exercise; please do not overthink things.

Take some time to think about what those four pillars are for your brand, and again fill in the template in your workbook. Do keep coming back to them, testing them, talking about them and trying them out. See what kind of conversations you can have and what difference it makes to how people engage with you and your brand.

We will be looking at this part again in part two of this book when you decide how to communicate your brand values and your brand messaging and how to tell your story and your narrative to make sure that you can do it in a way that resonates and connects with your ideal audience.

———

5

WHO ARE YOU HERE TO HELP?

So, you have found your thing. You are clear on what your purpose is and what your business does. You probably have an idea of the type of people who might want to buy your products or services. But how do you know who they really are, and why is it important to drill down and clarify who your ideal client is?

When we talk about your "ideal client", what we mean is those clients and customers who are more likely than others to buy your products and services from you.

When you start in business, it can be hard at first to know who the people are that will buy from you; in fact, at first, you are generally super happy that anyone is willing to pay for your products or services at all.

You have a rough idea of who it might be, but you don't know for sure. And the worst thing is the pressure from everyone else telling you that you need to get clear on what your ideal client avatar looks like. They want you to drill down and be as specific as you can. In other words, everyone is telling you to choose your niche and stick to it.

But inside your head, you are silently screaming. "I don't want to niche down; I want to sell my products and services to everyone. I want to sell to…. Well, basically anyone and everyone who'll buy from me."

To niche or not to niche!

Suppose your business is going to be teaching swimming lessons to children, like my client Puddle Ducks in Manchester and Worcestershire. In that case, you can be pretty confident that the people who are going to buy your swimming lessons will be people who have children who want or need to learn to swim. So, parents or carers of young children.

If your business is selling language services, particularly translation services, like my client Peak Translations, then you might imagine that companies looking to work and sell their products and services in other countries might require your services and buy from you. So, companies that export.

If you are a wedding photographer, it is obvious that your ideal clients are couples planning on getting married. So engaged couples.

You get my gist. It sounds straightforward, doesn't it? The owners of these three businesses could now go away and come up with a plan to attract as many of their ideal clients as possible.

However, they will find that the description of their ideal client is so vague, and the category is so huge that it is difficult to know whom they are talking to or how they can make a difference.

Let's look at it from another perspective, from the client's point of view. Imagine that you are going to run the London marathon next October and are looking for a fitness coach to help you go from couch to completing a marathon in just six months. You Google fitness instructors, and over one hundred different ones appear in the search. You can't possibly get in touch with all one hundred of them.

So, what are the criteria that will help you narrow down your search? What will you look for to help you choose? How could you be more specific in your search?

You might choose a location and whether you prefer to meet face to face or online. If it is the latter, then unless you want to pay a fortune or travel far each time for your session, you will look for somebody who is based near where you live or work.

Maybe you would prefer your instructor to be male or female?

What about their specialisms? Would you like to hire an instructor to help you with your general fitness levels? Or maybe you would prefer an instructor who specialises in helping you train to run long distances? Which do you think would help you be more successful?

Let's go back to our three earlier examples.

As a parent or carer looking for swimming lessons for their child, what kind of things would help them to choose? Location, price, age of the children in the classes, the method being taught, the type of lessons such as individual or group or maybe the experience or style of the teacher.

How about the business looking to export and needing translation services? What will help them to decide and choose the best supplier? Specific languages required, experience in their industry, the experience of the linguist, price per word?

And the wedding photographer? Style of photographs, type of package, location?

I am sure you will have heard the analogy about the heart surgeon or the generalist; I know whom I would rather have carry out open heart surgery on me if I ever need it.

So, when you look at things from your customer's perspective and put yourself in their shoes and think about how they make decisions, it becomes easier to understand the importance of getting clear about whom you want to help and why. Of course, the more specific you can be in identifying your ideal clients, the easier it will be for them to find you too.

And the more you can get to know them and get under their skin, the easier it will become for you to understand how they are feeling, what they need from you and how you can attract more of them to your business.

You can select your niche from various criteria such as geographical, quality, pricing, service type, customer type, and beliefs.... Maybe you have a combination of criteria that helps you to form your specific niche and positioning.

It sounds obvious, but make sure that the niche and position you choose is the right one. Just because you have identified a particular gap in the market for a specific niche does not mean that it is the right fit for you. Choose carefully and logically, bringing together all of your USPs, your zone of genius and experience and find the niche that best matches your skillset and the needs of that particular client.

I would like to make an important point here that can sometimes be forgotten as you get caught on that rollercoaster ride, and the need to make sales and grow intensifies.

We often hear the phrase 'the customer is always right', and although, as you will see in the next chapter, I am a huge believer in creating the most wonderful and memorable customer experiences for all your clients and delighting them at every step of the way. I don't want you ever to forget that as the business owner, you get to choose too!

What do I mean by that?

I mean that you get to choose the type of clients that you want to work with and that you want to attract to your business.

Obviously, I mean this from a completely ethical place and one of integrity, so of course, you must never discriminate against anybody. However, it is important to remember that you do not have to say yes to working with absolutely everybody. If you have a feeling about somebody or know that you will not be a good fit, then you should follow your instinct and say no. It will always be the right decision for both of you in the long run.

I want you to be intentional about choosing who your ideal client should be, and I will help you do this.

Before I take you through this process, just a quick side note for those who are in the beginning stages of building a business, I would suggest that you do not worry too much about this at first. You should concentrate on making those first sales in your business, proving your concept, and demonstrating that you have a viable business before focusing too much on drilling down.

And, as you will see. It is through trial and error, through working with and selling to different people, that you can test things out and understand what works well and what does not work so well.

———

Exercise: - Who are your ideal clients?

If you want to work out who your ideal clients are, here are some exercises that might help you. And if you already know who your ideal client is/are, I recommend carrying out this exercise anyway and checking in with yourself. Your brand will evolve, as will your clients, and this exercise is a great way to check in with yourself and tweak accordingly.

Firstly, make a list of your top ten clients and your ten worst clients and as you do, think about why you have added them to the respective lists. Then ask yourself these questions before giving them a score based on your answers.

NB: you will find a copy of this table in your downloadable workbook.

Are they easy to work with? Do they question your pricing? Can you deliver excellent service and results to them? Do they respect your boundaries, or do they overstep the mark time after time? How do they make you feel? What is the potential market volume of these types of clients?

By analysing them in this way, you can make an objective and subjective choice about the type of people you want to work with and the type of clients you want to attract to your business.

NB. If you have a partner or team, then I would highly recommend carrying out this exercise with them and taking on board their answers to the questions in your decision making.

Client	Ease of working with them	Value for money	Joy / PITA tax (Pain In The A**E)

———

Very often though, you will find that after time your niche will find you. You will find that certain types of people will naturally gravitate more easily towards you because of your style, your personality or your approach.

For me, I started out working with "small businesses", which is a vast category, but actually, when you dig deeper and look at the hundreds of business owners that I have helped and supported over the last seven years, the majority of them have similar values to me. They come from a place of integrity and are very much purpose-led; they want to create a business that they love and make an impact and a difference to their customers.

Most are women, all are owner-led, and a lot are family-owned businesses run by an in-house husband-and-wife team.

This will evolve too. You will find your niche expands as your client base and your brand grows. You will adapt your offering to meet your clients' ever-changing demands and stay relevant and focused.

And don't forget. Just because you are being specific in your niche and your position in the market does not mean that you can't work with other types of clients or offer additional services.

I know many of my clients fear that becoming known as the 'go-to' brand for a particular niche means closing the door on other clients or other products and services. This is simply not true. You are being specific and niche enough to be the expert and the obvious choice in your field to attract your customers to you. You can still do other things; you just might not shout about them as much. And don't forget that your brand will naturally evolve as you grow and become more successful, adding new products and services and expanding your market potential.

My wonderful mastermind member Rachel Spencer has developed a very successful business by focusing on a specific niche, publicity for pet businesses. A journalist by trade, Rachel identified a gap in the market that resonated with her passion, skills and experience and has since built a successful business helping pet business owners across the UK to get into the press and create awareness for their brands.

Now, in 2022, she is looking to expand her niche and offer her clients a different kind of service and support. She has recognised that one of the key drivers for her clients in getting the results they need is to have the confidence, the right mindset and be bold enough to put themselves out there, and so Rachel has recently developed a course to help them in this area.

So, niching down does not mean staying in the same place forever more. It is about leveraging what you do best, focusing on how you can help your clients and staying awake and listening, ready to grow and evolve as your clients and industry do—making sure you are ahead of the game.

Jeff Bezos is the perfect example of someone with a clear niche who began selling books online in his back bedroom. Amazon today is the 'go-to' brand for all online shopping worldwide with an annual global turnover of 470bn dollars.

Creating your customer avatar

As you define who your ideal client is, I encourage you to be as specific as possible. The more detailed you can be at this stage, the more appropriate you can be in your communications and marketing and in ensuring that you meet their expectations and deliver time after time.

The easiest and simplest way to do this is to use an example of an existing client, the top scoring client from the previous exercise, and use them to build your customer avatar or profile.

Now please remember that this is not going to be an exact science, and there will always be exceptions to the rule. But I promise that the closer you get to your identifying your ideal client will help you in all aspects of building your brand further down the line.

Some people might find that you need to create several different customer avatars because you have other product streams, markets, or service offerings that you work with, and that is ok too.

Something is better than nothing, so start with one and create more as you need to.

Get under the skin of your ideal client.

The more you can get under the skin of your ideal client, the more value and better experience you will be able to provide. I encourage you to get to know them inside out, every detail from where they live to what they do for a living, to what they like to eat or how they like to spend their Saturdays.

The better you can understand them, their challenges, their problems, and their needs, the better you will be able to communicate and engage with them and, of course, encourage them to buy from you.

I want you to get to know your ideal client so well that when you are talking to them about their life and their world, when you are creating content and tools and resources for them, they feel like you have been inside their head, because what you are saying and doing resonates so much.

Begin by filling in the basic information that you can see in the table in the workbook. This is the generic customer mapping profiler that you will find in most marketing textbooks.

	Customer 1 - Name	Customer 2 - Name	Customer 3 - Name
Gender			
Age			
Geographic			
Education			
Work / Income			
Interests / Hobbies			
Digital Activities			
Spending			
Purchase Behaviour			
What clinches the deal?			

However, I don't want you to stop there. I want you to deep dive into their lives and get under their skin, and the best way to find out this kind of information is to ask them.

I suggest simply starting by getting to know them first as individuals, asking questions, being genuinely interested in them, and listening to what they say, what they share and the type of questions they ask. This will all be valuable in the long term as you create and build relationships with them.

You can use various methods to conduct further research, such as focus groups with your existing clients, either face to face or online, or customer feedback forms using Google forms or Survey Monkey, where you can ask them specific questions about themselves and their experience.

Find out what is important to them, what keeps them awake at night, and what their goals and objectives are. What are they struggling with, or simply what makes them laugh?

I suggest you think about this as a game, and it's your job to find out everything you can possibly know about them. What makes them tick, what they love to eat, what they listen to in the shower and more.

The more you can understand them, the more you can get under their skin, the easier it will be to serve them and to help them. You want to know so much about them that when you communicate with them, they can't believe it and feel like you can read their minds.

Another great way to find out more about them is to connect with them on their social media channels and look out for what they are sharing and liking, the types of conversations they are having and what they are talking about. The types of groups they have joined and the other pages or handles that they follow.

Once you have collated all your data and information, you need to find an effective way to store it and be able to use it for your communications and marketing moving forward.

This could be something as simple as an Excel spreadsheet or you could invest in your very own **CRM** *Customer Relationship Management* tool to help you to stay on top of things. We will talk more about CRMs and how to use them in part 3 of this book.

Keeping your clients at the forefront of your mind is key, and thinking about them, their needs and what they expect from you throughout all aspects of your business is going to help you to deliver again and again.

––––––––

Exercise: - Bringing it all together.

To help you keep focused with this, I recommend you gather all the information you have on your chosen ideal client, and you create a persona poster.

Build your ideal client's persona, either based on one specific existing client or make one up based on all the information you have collated.

Find a photo, write the description and capture all the details and things you know about that person.

Put the poster in a prominent place in your office or near your desk and refer back to it at all times.

––––––––

Why should they choose you?

So now that you have worked out who you want to work with and the type of people you want to attract. What is it about you and your brand that is going to make them choose you instead of your competition?

This is where we need to look at what makes you special and stand out from the crowd and why it is important to look at things from your client's perspective.

————

Exercise: - Why should your ideal clients choose you?

I want you to identify and define your USP or Unique Selling Proposition.

Traditionally, this is where you, as a business owner, will make a huge list of everything you think makes you unique and why your ideal clients should buy from you. However, this time, I want you to try it differently and start by putting yourself in your customers' shoes.

Using the table as a guide, and if you have downloaded the workbook from my website, you will have access to the template.

I want you to think about that Google search again and consider what your people will be looking for when they are looking for a product or service like yours and start to list the attributes in the far-left hand column.

Then I want you to go back to the previous chapter and select items that add value to your brand and that make you unique.

Think about your CV of life, your values and your purpose and pillars, which ones do you need to add to the list below?

USP (Unique Selling proposition)	Description	So what?
Family-owned business	They are a husband-and-wife team, the two sons also work for the business.	They have strong family values; the business is at the heart of the family so that must mean that they really care about the success of the business and so will go above and beyond. We can trust them to deliver.
Quality certification ISO 9001	They have quality accreditation by the ISO body.	The products and manufacturing processes meet the recognised quality standard, which means that I can have peace of mind that they are safe and will deliver and perform as they should.
Made in Britain	Part of the Made In Britain organisation	I can trust the products; they have been manufactured in the UK. I can trust them because they are associated with the Made In Britain brand which recognises UK manufacturing. It aligns with my values and what is important to me as I want to support UK businesses, the economy and market.

There are no wrong answers, and please don't overthink this exercise. The more things you can identify and note down, the better. I encourage my clients to have at least twenty-five different items on there that demonstrate their uniqueness.

Once you have completed the table, I want you to add a description next to each item in the second column. Being as detailed as you can and providing as much information as possible. And then, finally, you are going to think about your customer and try and work out what that means to them. I want you to ask yourself literally, and so what? Why should they care?

Here is when we need to understand what is important to them and what they are thinking about.

So, as you can see in the example above.

Once you have completed this exercise, you will have your very own personalised bank of content and messaging for your brand marketing and communication.

It is important to note here also that you don't have to find things that are entirely unique to you and your brand and that you won't find with your competitors. Sometimes it can be the most obvious things that help you to stand out simply because others assume that customers know about them and take them for granted.

As in the example that is taken from one of my clients, Autac, who manufactures electrical retractable cables for use across many different industries; ISO quality accreditation is important. And although most cable manufacturers will probably be accredited, most don't talk about it in their communication and marketing. Autac has chosen quality to be one of its four key brand pillars and intentionally uses this to its advantage, sharing with its clients and potential clients the benefits and importance of the accreditation and the quality process within their products and services and therefore differentiating themselves from their competition in terms of quality.

———

PART 2

COMMUNICATION

6

BUILDING TRUST

I could not write a book about future-proofing your business without talking to you about the importance of trust. So, I hope you don't mind, but I have included this short chapter here from me to give you some food for thought and hopefully get you thinking differently about the way you and your brand interact with your customers, your teams, your audience, and any other key partner.

What is trust, and what can we do to earn more of it?

Ken Blanchard identifies four key components in his ABCD Trust model. I think this is an insightful model that helps us understand the key elements that come into play when we are looking to develop and grow trust with the people around us. The model was created to help leaders within organisations build trust with their employees and teams. However, I believe that the four components are equally relevant to small businesses and brands that are looking to grow trust and goodwill with customers and their teams.

1. **Ability** - this is when you show people that you can do the job or work that needs to be done. You can look after the project, get the results, or you have the skills required. Are you an expert in your field or industry? This is where you can demonstrate that you know what you're doing and why people should listen to you or want to work with you.

2. **Believable** - are you authentic and genuine? This is where people will either believe what you say or do or not, and they'll check whether you're being honest and transparent with them. Do you act with integrity and respect, or are you trying to be something you're not? Sometimes being authentic and sharing your rollercoaster ride can help to show your human side and make you more believable.

3. **Connected** - this comes down to building those relationships. Do you show you care? And do people believe that you care? Listening is a great way to connect and build rapport with your teams and customers. People love to talk about themselves, and if you can ask questions and ask for feedback and make it as personal to them as possible, you can build trust.

4. **Are you Dependable?** - which means do you do what you say you're going to do? How well can people rely on you? Do you maintain the levels of quality that you promise? This can also be linked to consistency and whether you show up when you say you're going to in the way that is in keeping with you and your brand.

As you know, I am a massive advocate of people in business. I believe that everything comes down to the relationships and rapport that we have with one another, and an essential factor within this is your ability to show up as your true authentic self.

One of my pet hates is when I see a brand pretending to be something that it is not. I don't believe they are intentionally misleading people or being dishonest. Instead, I think it comes from an outdated view that small businesses and their brands need to be "corporate" and "stuffy" or need to appear to be bigger than they are.

I often see brands that I know behind the scenes are sole traders or one-man bands, using the term 'we' in their messaging. Now I completely understand where they are coming from; I used to do it myself in the earlier years of my business. I was afraid that people would not take me seriously, would not consider working with me, and would think less of me if I showed up as myself and told the real story.

Learning to be myself and be honest about it has probably been one of the hardest things I have ever had to do. I still find it hard sometimes today, and I know that many of my clients struggle too.

However, I genuinely believe that if you can learn to do this, to show up as your own genuine self, the good, the bad and the ugly, then I believe that this will make all the difference in building trust and future-proofing your business.

 "Find out who you are and do it on purpose."

DOLLY PARTON

Fast forward seven years, and I have fully embraced the fact that I am the face of my brand; I am proud to talk about my business, and I own the fact that it is just me. I work with hundreds of small business owners across businesses of different shapes and sizes, and I also work as a partner to some very big corporate organisations too. And they know it's just me.

Although today, I want to share that I am so grateful for my amazing virtual team of people who work behind the scenes and help me to manage all the different projects and tasks. Thank you, Kirsty, Tracey, Tanya, Melanie, Dave, James, Rebecca and Clare.

I think the point I want to make is that times have changed, and we live in a very different world, and I believe that small business owners and entrepreneurs like you are highly regarded within the world of business.

There is a natural movement to support small businesses and value what you each have to offer, which, as you know, differs incredibly from corporate organisations for many reasons, including expertise, customer service, creativity, going above and beyond, flexibility, experience, and the list goes on.

I also think that a significant factor that comes into play and is forgotten too readily is that behind every email and job title in big organisations is a real human being who loves to work with interesting people like you and wants to support brands like yours.

"When you're delivering a presentation, a workshop or a speech or whatever it might be, to be really effective and ensure you turn up in the right way, you need to think to yourself that you're there to share and tell what you know and avoid being one of those people who just show up to take."

SIMON SINEK.

Even if being yourself can be scary, I think Simon is right; if you remind yourself that you are there to give, it profoundly changes the way you show up, the words you choose and the way you interact with your audience. Ultimately, it is not about you! This also helps those of you who, if you are anything like me, get horrendous butterflies and nerves before each session. By making it about your audience and not you, it takes away the pressure; you are there to help those in front of you and to add value.

Finally, every brand deserves a face. You know how hard it is to trust someone if you can't see their face. Well, it's exactly the same for your brand. We need to know who is behind the brand, what you stand for and why you do what you do before we can decide whether or not we can trust you. This means creating your About Us and your introduction, adding photos and letting us know who you are. Sharing your story and some behind-the-scenes content with us, and if you're feeling brave, let us in a little bit into your world so that we can get to know you more and decide whether we like you and ultimately if we want to trust you enough to buy from you.

I am not saying you need to be creating videos on TikTok or going live every morning on Instagram; however, allowing your audience to get a feel for you, to know that you are there, and demonstrate that you have a strategy and that you are in control will help you enormously in creating trust and goodwill, which is exactly what you need to help you to future-proof your business.

———

Exercise:

Ask yourself these questions and simply note down what comes up for you.

- How often do you show up as your true self?
- In what situations are you more likely to be yourself?
- What do you notice?

I would also like to encourage you to notice how you react and engage with different brands and businesses and identify what you need to know, see or feel before you are ready to buy from or engage with a brand. How do you feel if you don't know who's behind the brand?

———

7

BRINGING YOUR BRAND TO LIFE

Now that you have got clear on your vision, your purpose and what you stand for, it's time to start being creative and bringing your brand to life.

It is time to find your voice, to tell your story and to communicate in such a way that you can become a real magnet that attracts the right kind of people to you. I want you to be able to build trust and goodwill through everything you do and exceed people's expectations every time, delighting them every step of the way.

How you communicate will be key in helping you establish yourself as a brand and a business that people know, love and trust. Being intentional about it from the start enables you to create consistency and clarity in what you stand for and become recognisable wherever you show up and whatever you are doing.

It is important to start creating and developing your brand experience and managing your customers' expectations as soon as possible and in the best possible way.

Before you start to think about your business and brand, I would like you to take a moment to consider and look at some of the other brands out there.

Waitrose is a great example. (You've got to love Waitrose!)

Have you noticed that whichever Waitrose store you visit, whether in Buxton in the Peak District or next to the Menai bridge on the Isle of Anglesey, you will always find the same look and feel? You just 'know' you are in a Waitrose store, sometimes without seeing a sign that says Waitrose.

What do I mean by this? Well, Waitrose has a clear and distinct visual brand identity with a defined palette of colours, a particular typeface, and a way of designing its packaging and marketing material that is recognisable. It is more than just the logo. From the Essentials Waitrose packaging to the recipe cards available in store to the Waitrose customer newspaper, everything has a specific look and feel to it that is consistent across the board and instantly recognisable to its customers.

Exercise:

Can you think of three of your favourite brands and answer these questions for each one?

- Why have you chosen this brand?
- What is it about this brand that you like?

Think about the customer experience you had with them.

- What was it that sparked your interest in the beginning?
- How long did it take before you liked them and trusted them enough to buy from them?
- What was the buying experience like? Try to remember what happened at all stages of the journey, from simply browsing to receiving your product or service and then the aftercare that followed.
- How did it make you feel?
- Would you buy from that brand again?

Now think about another three brands, but this time choose ones that you don't like and answer the same questions noting down what it is that you don't like.

When you have finished, compare your two lists, and notice anything that jumps out at you.

- What are the key takeaways from this?
- What can you apply to your brand and business?

─────

Brand identity - the visual part.

This is the bit where many people get confused and get themselves into a bit of a muddle. People often think about the logo and the visual aspect when we talk about the word brand. However, your brand is much more than that, as we discussed in Part 1, and the visual element is in fact, there to support and reinforce your brand, which starts with you, your vision, and your values. Remember, your brand is what distinguishes your business from another.

I recommend finalising Part 1 of this book before you start to work on your visual identity, as everything you choose should be based upon your brand's natural essence and foundations.

The same goes for you if you want to refresh or update your brand. Always go back to Part 1 of this book and revise and develop your brand vision first before deciding on changes to your brand identity, core messaging or key tools such as your website.

It will make everything so much easier for yourself and for the creative partners that you work with in the future. If you can give them as much detail as possible about your brand foundations and everything we looked at in Part 1, then they will be able to get to work more effectively, and the whole process will be much easier and simpler. They won't have to guess, use trial and error or spend too much time going back and forth with you to check in because they will already have a clear vision and roadmap from you about what your brand stands for, what you are trying to achieve and what you need from them.

Get your brand identity finalised before you begin working on any of your collateral or website, as if not, you will find that you are reinventing the wheel at every turn, and the consistency and quality will be lost. I have seen so many business owners get this the wrong way around, and it can become a painful process on all sides.

Taking some time to get clear on your brand identity is important in establishing yourself as a trusted brand. However, please do not fall into the easy trap of getting caught up in too many details, allowing perfectionism to take hold and stop you from moving forward.

I know that it can be super hard at first to get yourself over the line, to start making those sales, and there is a real balance to find in getting yourself organised, choosing your logo, brand toolkit and colours and then not spending a fortune on things you don't need. If in doubt, then tell yourself you don't need it. You don't, I promise!

The thing to remember when it comes down to your brand visual identity and logo is that nobody gets it one hundred per cent right the first time, and you probably won't ever be completely satisfied with it, and that's ok. As your business evolves, so will your brand, your logo, and your toolkit. As I'm writing this book, I am undergoing my fourth brand update in just seven years!

I know many people who spent absolute fortunes on high-ticket branding packages and snazzy websites in their first few months of business. They spent so much money and time trying to look the part that they forgot about the most essential part of running a business, which is building relationships and selling their products and services. Unfortunately, many of them ran out of precious cash and didn't make it past the six-month mark.

Once you have become more established, and of course, if you do have the funds to invest in a proper graphic designer who can get under the skin of your business and help you to create the visuals that represent your vision and brand, then go for it.

However, there are many great options available now for you to do it yourself and to an acceptable standard with a small budget. Some tools are even free to a certain point, such as the design website CANVA where you can make everything you need yourself, from creating your own logo, designing your own marketing collateral, and producing e-books.*

(*Just a word of caution when using these kinds of sites for your business, please be aware of any hidden copyright issues).

The hybrid approach

In my business today, I use a mixture of professional graphic designers who develop my brand identity, create the key assets, and design anything high-ticket that I want to print or that I need to look its best, like the cover of this book for example or my website. And then, I invest in professional templates that I can then upload into my CANVA portfolio to update myself and reuse time after time for things like social media content and email marketing.

However you choose to go about defining your visual brand identity, you should make sure that once complete, you have a clear set of guidelines that you can refer back to each time that describes the specific font choices, colours, styles of images and any important instructions that need to be included. You should also request a set of all your key assets and creative files in the most appropriate and relevant format.

Not only will this allow you to become clear on how you should implement and use your new brand identity, but it also ensures that you have complete control and have everything you need for the future so that you are free to work with who you want. You do not want to be dependent on or tied into working with a previous graphic designer if you choose not to be. In other words, you are future-proofing your brand identity.

NB: You can find an example of my brand guidelines to give you an idea of what this should look like within your free downloadable workbook.

Defining your Brand Tone of Voice

Once your visual identity is finalised, it's time to start thinking about your brand voice. This is how you are going to speak and show up to your audience and will once again need to be consistent across all your communications. Whether that be written promotional copy on your website, how you or your team talk to your customers directly, how you answer your phone, how you write and sign off emails or letters and how you show up on social media.

––––––

Exercise: - Tone of Voice

NB: You will find the Tone of Voice template for your brand inside your downloadable workbook.

To prepare for this, I recommend that you refer back to Chapter 3 in this book and revisit your vision and values.

And then, remind yourself about your ideal clients and answer the following questions before you begin.

- How do you want people to perceive you?
- How do you want your customers to feel when they are engaging with your brand?
- What are they looking for from you?

There is no right or wrong answer to this, just keep your customers in mind and consider their needs.

Start by listing your values in the left-hand column and think about what each one means in style and personality for your brand. Define for yourself and others what each characteristic means and then work out the dos and don'ts in terms of behaviours behind each one.

Value characteristic	Description	Dos	Don'ts
Approachable	We are warm and welcoming and easy to approach. We want customers and other stakeholders to feel at ease, able to talk and engage with us and feel comfortable.	Smile, open body language to be welcoming. Use less formal language and easy to understand Use plain English Ask questions Take your time to engage.	Make people feel uncomfortable No jargon No complicated or long sentences

In other words, remind yourself why you have chosen that particular value and what you want your customers to take away from it. Then think about what that means in terms of the way you need to behave and communicate.

The dos and don'ts are an excellent way for you to get super clear on how you should and shouldn't engage with your customers and what that means for your brand and your team.

As the example shows, if it's important for your brand to come across as 'approachable', then making sure you are friendly is key. You would intentionally use easy-to-understand language and you would smile and be welcoming with your body language. Avoiding jargon would be important, as would making a conscious effort to engage, have a conversation and answer all the questions.

I highly recommend taking the time to fill out this tool and keeping it to hand as you develop your brand. It will be incredibly useful to refer back to as a guide as you write any copy or marketing communications and as you onboard any new team members or engage with partners who will be acting under your brand. If you do already have a team, then I highly recommend involving them in this process; it might provide you with a few surprises too!

Defining your Brand messaging

In Chapter 4, you looked at your four brand pillars that pull together the main themes that represent your brand. These are the foundations for your brand messaging, content, and all communications you will create to represent your brand moving forward.

As with all aspects of your brand, they will develop and evolve as your brand grows and matures, and the same will happen to your messaging. Particularly as you test the different pillars and see how they land with your audience and how they feel with you.

Other things to consider as you build your brand foundations are any key phrases, frameworks, or words that you might use frequently or that people identify with you and your brand.

For example, for me, lots of my clients remember and repeat my most common phrases back to me such as: Stop being selfish; what *would Lucy do? It's all about Communication! An Inside Out Approach, The TripAdvisor effect,* and of course, *Clarity, Communication and Connection and future-proofing your business.*

Exercise:- Note down your key phrases or words.

If you are unsure what yours might be, reach out to your clients or partners and ask them if they can tell you what your recognisable phrases or sayings are. Maybe you could listen back to yourself when you deliver and record a workshop or presentation and see if you can identify any special straplines or ways of saying things that are unique to you and your brand.

———

Thinking about your Brand touches

If you know me, then you will know that I am all about the little things and the personal touch. Whether that is in my business or outside of it, I will be talking more about the little things you can do to embellish your customer experience later in the book.

In this chapter though, I would like to encourage you to think about the little touches you can add to your brand to help bring it to life and make it more memorable for your audience. This can be anything you want it to be, as long as it fits with your brand, values, and vision.

For example, my brand touches are linked to the fact that I believe in 'less is more' and, of course, that also I love wearing red lipstick. I'm renowned for always dressing head to toe in black, but then I add a splash of red lipstick to my lips. With my graphic designer, we have replicated this and incorporated a splash of red into my branding that I use sparingly across my brand or if I want to accentuate something special to me, such as this book!

I have become known for always using red pencils when I'm working and writing. I have also extracted the house symbol that sits within my logo, which represents me sitting at the heart of my clients' businesses, and I use it across my different content and collateral, whether that is for social media, on post-cards or any other literature that I create. By consistently using this symbol, and of course, my brand colours, fonts and style, people can recognise my brand even though I am not using my logo.

Over the years, I have also brought some of these brand touches to life in the form of postcards to welcome new clients, beautiful notebooks and red pencils as gifts or useful tools such as planners or workbooks that are all mini versions of my brand.

I love being creative like this, having some fun and being able to create an experience for my clients at the same time.

––––––

Exercise:- What are your brand touches?

Note down some ideas you could develop as your brand touches to bring your brand to life and engage with your clients.

––––––

8

TELLING STORIES

There is a reason why people love stories so much. Whether that is fairy tales, thrillers, true or made-up stories, we all love to get comfy and listen to a good story, and storytelling has existed since the beginning of time.

Children for generations have learned right from wrong, good against evil and who to trust or not all through a variety of storytelling such as fairy tales like Little Red Riding Hood or stories about religion or folklore. What we often don't think about are the stories we hear from our parents, family and friends, teachers, or neighbours that, without realising it, have influenced us in some way and helped to make us the way we are today.

But what is it about stories that makes us love them so much?

Stories are a way for us to share information, connect, help people understand, create meaning and inspire and build trust with each other.

Why is storytelling so important for your brand?

By telling a story in such a way, you can create relatable content that resonates with people and makes them feel connected. You can communicate your message, demonstrate how you help people and let people in under the surface of your brand to encourage them to get to know, like and trust you.

What makes a good story?

A good story has a clear structure, with a start, a middle and an end. There are clearly defined characters, a setting, a plot, the conflict and of course, the resolution or, as we know it, the happy ending. And a great story is one that resonates, encourages the reader to connect with the character(s) and the situation(s) and makes them feel empathy and emotion.

How can you share what you do and how good you are without feeling icky?

So many of my clients talk to me about this, and I am sure that you can relate; and sometimes you have felt the same; I know I have and still do sometimes. You don't want to put yourself out there, and you don't want to talk about the great results you are getting for your clients or how amazing your products and services are because you don't want to seem like you are showing off or being too brazen.

I don't know. Maybe there is something about the way we are brought up or maybe it is because we are being very *British*? From a very early age we are taught that it is an excellent quality to be modest. That it is not polite or *the done thing* to go round telling everyone how wonderful we are, that is known as 'bragging'!

Ok, but that does not help you though, does it?

If you want to make your business a success and attract more of the right kind of clients, you need to find a way to let people know about you and your products and services. A way to let them know how you can help them and, most importantly, enable them to see why they need you.

You have to stop being selfish!

If you hide away, if you don't share your gifts, your passion, and your business with the world, then how can the people who really need you, find out about you?

How can you help people, and how can you ultimately grow a successful business if you don't want to put yourself out there?

I am sorry if I sound a bit shouty and harsh here, I am only teasing you a little bit!

But seriously, there are people out there who need your products and services, and the only way they will find out about you is if you communicate with them and let them know you exist and show them how you can help them.

One of the best ways to get started with this and to begin sharing your success stories is to capture, create and share your own "YODA moments".

What on earth is a YODA moment?

If you don't know it already, then you should be aware that I am a huge Star Wars fan, and I have been since I was very small. In fact, I can remember meeting Darth Vadar in Toy and Hobby when I was just five years old, and I still have his signed autograph to prove it!

Anyway, if you're not a Star Wars fan yourself, then please don't worry! For this exercise, I'd like you to think about one of your favourite movies or books and see if you can identify the character who was there behind the scenes, the guide, the mentor, or the teacher. The one who was there to help the hero to overcome evil and save the world.

Yoda is an old Jedi Master who teaches Luke Skywalker, the hero, to learn the 'Force', overcome the baddie Darth Vadar and save the universe from the evil Empire.

You might have chosen Dumbledore in Harry Potter, the Fairy Godmother in Cinderella, or Miss Honey in Matilda.

I want you to start thinking of yourself and your brand as YODA, the guide, the teacher and the support that works your magic behind the scenes and enables your clients, the heroes, to win the day and overcome their challenges and succeed.

By creating your own YODA moment stories, you can show the value you add to your clients but in a non-icky way. You can describe how you help and all the excellent work you do through your stories, and you can build awareness for and promote your clients at the same time!

When I talk about my 121 mentoring programmes to potential clients, I share a story about one of my mentees, Emily, who is studying for a digital marketing apprenticeship. Taking on a marketing apprentice was a risk for Helen, the MD at Peak, who has little or no experience in marketing. How could she support Emily properly and ensure that the business' marketing continued effectively, bringing in the leads they needed?

Emily joined my 121 programme in September, which gave Helen peace of mind that she would have the support she needed, then fast forward twelve months of working with me intensively each week, and Emily has been able to come into her own. She has grown in confidence and has been able to transform the way Peak communicates as a business and brand. She is now able to design and critically evaluate her own marketing campaigns and strategy. Their social media channels have grown by 200% with their ideal clients, and she is about to go live with the new company website she has been project managing.

My clients Kim and Greg, who run an events company, HDK, have fallen in love with their business again and have a pipeline of work for the next twelve months, more enquiries than ever before, and they are now expanding and thinking about taking on staff.

They had survived the covid pandemic, but they were shattered and weary, and although they had a steady trickle of clients, they were not convinced that the business was viable or even if they wanted to continue. They invested in some 121 strategic support with me, and we revisited what makes them tick, redefined their brand vision and values, and created a strategy and roadmap to move them forward. They now feel in control, focused and really positive about the future.

Finally, how proud am I to celebrate the success of my clients, husband and wife team David and Sallie Lowe from Autac Products! Over the last three years, we have worked together to develop a new brand identity and a marketing and communications strategy that has helped them to revolutionise their business and take them from a £2.5M turnover to £5M at the end of 2022.

By putting your clients' successes first, you take the ickiness away, and you can focus on communicating the results you are helping them to achieve and describe the work that you do behind the scenes.

––––––

Exercise:

Take some time out to think about and capture some of your own **YODA** moments. How have you helped your clients, and what are the stories you could tell about them?

NB: You'll find some space in the FREE downloadable workbook.

––––––

Creating engaging content

"Have I told you the story about my 'MELON' man?

He just knew which would be the PERFECT melon for me, would you?

I lived in France for ten years, and one of my favourite things to do every Saturday morning would be to go to the local market. It was an experience from the start, with beautiful sights and smells of fresh bread, roast chickens, cheese, meats, and of course, the absolutely wonderful freshly picked, in-season fruit and vegetables.

Visiting the market was serious stuff because, as you know, the French take their food very seriously!

My favourite stall though, and the one that I always saved until last, was the man selling melons. I loved it because firstly, he only sold melons (or he may have had some garlic and a few tomatoes too). Secondly, he made me understand just how important it is to know your melon and treat it with respect. Finally, he always had a plate of juicy slices for us to taste, he genuinely made choosing my melon an absolute delight!

"Quand est-ce vous allez le manger, votre melon?" ("When will you be eating your melon?") he would ask.

Sometimes it would be later that day, or sometimes for Sunday lunch; it didn't matter when it was or what I replied because what happened next was the secret.

He would carefully pick up each melon from his box, have a smell, a squeeze and a good look, and choose THE melon that he knew would be just perfect for me. Not too ripe, not too hard, just right!

He was the perfect business owner,

✔ he had chosen a great niche and specialism

✔ he was the go-to melon man

✔ he was an expert in his product

✔ he attracted more customers with his plate of melon slices, letting us get a taste of his product or service

✔ he asked questions and listened

and then

✔ he found THE perfect melon for my needs which meant I would go back time after time!

Using analogies and telling stories is probably my favourite and most effective way of creating engaging content. I shared my melon man story a few years ago to my FREE group and across my socials, and I still have people refer to it today or remind me about him. It is super powerful stuff!

Communicate with Purpose

If you take away just ONE thing from this section of the book, *Communication*, I want you to remember to always 'Communicate with Purpose'.

As a small business owner, I know that you don't always have the luxury of time, which means that you have no time to waste either.

So, when you sit down to think about your messaging and what you want to communicate with your customers, potential customers, and wider audience, I want you to be super intentional about it.

What do I mean by being intentional?

Everything must reflect your vision, business goals, and objectives.

In other words, I want you to ask yourself each time, what are you trying to achieve? And why are you doing what you are doing?

It sounds super simple and obvious doesn't it? Most of my clients laugh at me now and repeat back to me, "But why?!" Because I am constantly bringing them back to this and challenging them on each aspect of their business. It is so important to focus on the right things, and we can easily get distracted or caught up doing lots of other things, spinning lots of plates and not moving forward because we have lost track of why we are doing it.

Get into the habit of asking yourself why, especially when it comes to your communication, whomever you want to communicate with. Be clear on why you are doing it, what you want to achieve and how you are going to achieve it.

Ask yourself why you are creating this piece of content today, why you are writing that email or creating that particular post for Facebook or TikTok. Decide what your goal is and then what your Call To Action (CTA) needs to be. What action do you want your audience to take after engaging with your content?

Now I don't want you to overthink it either or overcomplicate things. Your goal might simply be that you want them to get to know, like and trust you more, so you are telling them a story about how you became an expert in your field. In that case, the

CTA might simply be to get them to engage with you and join in your conversation.

If your goal is to grow your email list, then you need to think about the type of content that will encourage your ideal clients to give you their email address and how you can continue to add value and nurture them once they have signed up.

Or maybe you want to become the "go-to" business for insights and knowledge about a particular industry, so people will come to you for assistance when they need it. In that case, developing regular updates, blog articles, videos or how-to guides offering free and value add content will be most appropriate. Again, you might want to consider how you can engage with your audience further through conversation, polls or offering high value add in exchange for their email address.

Go back to Chapters 4 and 7 and remind yourself of your brand messaging, your four brand pillars and your brand tone of voice.

Have your ideal client profile to hand and create your content with them in mind. Speak directly to them and talk to them as if it was just you and them in the room. This is precisely what I do when I write my weekly emails to my audience or when I post on social media or go live, I literally imagine that I am speaking to my ideal client. If it is an email, I will begin by writing dear Ellie and if it is video, I will have them in my mind as I speak.

This is also a great way to overcome the fear factor of getting yourself out there by focusing on that one individual.

But remember, you are not here just to create nice content; you are here to grow your business and your brand. Remember that this is a long game and that business is all about people, relationships, goodwill, and trust. In my opinion, good value-add content is the key.

Creating excellent and engaging content is essential for:

- Creating a connection between you and your audience
- Helping you to build and nurture relationships
- Building awareness for your brand and what you do
- Helping with your organic search and enables you to rank higher on Google and other search engines
- Developing goodwill, trust, and brand loyalty
- Driving people to where you want them to go, your website or other.
- Saving you time and energy
- And, of course, making sales

What is 'good' content?

I believe that good content enables you to achieve your goals. Good content is based on your ideal client, has your audience in mind and is focused on adding value at all times.

Think about making your content:

Engaging - you want it to catch people's attention and stop them when they are scrolling.

Shareable - you want to encourage people to share your content so that you can get in front of new people. And don't forget that you can curate, recreate or share other people's content that you think will be of interest to your audience. Just don't forget to credit and mention the author.

Saveable - Creating useful content that your audience wants to save is great for the algorithm as it demonstrates high-quality content. Think about this when you are designing your content, what would make people want to refer back to or keep a post or article for later?

Signposting - By signposting your audience to other relevant and appropriate content, events, or businesses, you add value, demonstrate you are credible and join in conversations and engage with other brands in your field.

To add value - this should be a given every time. With your ideal client in mind, you want to help them with a problem, provide solutions or insights, be thought-provoking or challenging or simply make them smile. It doesn't have to be educational or formal every time, sometimes your audience might need some downtime, inspiration or just a good laugh!

Hit the mark - you want your audience to feel like you are a mind-reader, and you know exactly what is on their mind and what they are thinking about. And remember, it does not always have to be about your brand and what you do; in fact that would be incredibly boring if it was don't you think?

So how do you know what to talk about in your content?

There are many different methods and ways to organise your content and each coach or teacher has their own way of doing things. I have learned from lots of different people over the last seven years, and the following six objectives are a combination of what I have learned, tried and tested and developed to use in my own content and from seeing the results my clients have had with theirs. In your downloadable workbook you can find a list of my recommendations for further reading and extra resources in case you'd like to dig a bit deeper.

For now, I believe that a great way to start and get yourself going is to keep these six objectives in mind:

1. **Awareness** - share content about your industry, specialist field, and sector. This can be educational, building awareness for your passion.
2. **Connection** - this is about creating content that connects and resonates with people, letting them know more about your brand, about you and about why you do what you do. You can share content from your brand pillars, and talk about your purpose and vision and your Lego bricks. Don't forget that people love to see what is happening behind the scenes, share some insights into your personal life, and let them see how you work or what you get up to throughout the day. People love soap operas and reality shows, you can tap into this with your content.
3. **Expertise** - this is the place for you to demonstrate that you do know what you are talking about. You are the expert in your field, and your products and services are the right ones for your clients. Think about adding value, how-to guides, resources, and informative pieces that educate your audience and answer any questions they may have or solve any problems or challenges they face.
4. **Build relationships** - this is where you want to think about engaging with your audience. Think about

it like you want to move from chatting with them in your front garden to inviting them round into your back garden for a cup of tea and a chat. Start the conversation, make it more personal and create relationships. Encourage people to DM (Direct Message) you, join your free group, add comments on your posts, download your resources and tools, give you their email address, and jump on a call.

5. **Have Fun!** - be yourself, be true to your brand and values and enjoy it! Remember we talked about the energy that you can bring to the room. This is just as important online and through any content that you create. You want your people to feel good when they interact with you and your brand. So have fun, smile and be authentic.

6. **Sales** – don't forget to let people know how they can work with you or how they can buy your products or services. And make sure you do this from an early stage and then consistently as you move forward.

How to plan your content?

When I am mentoring my clients, I recommend that they do this quarterly and create a ninety-day rolling plan for their content. This is so that you can be more proactive and ensure that your content supports your business strategy and roadmap, and by planning ahead, it means you are no longer shooting from the hip. You feel more in control, and your content will naturally become more effective.

Just like magazines and other key publications, thinking ahead and planning out your editorial months in advance will allow you to ensure your content is good and of value, and it will take the pressure off you as a business owner.

I suggest that you block some time in your diary every ninety days to plan and map out your content for the next quarter.

Start by thinking about your goals and roadmap for the three months ahead. What is happening in your business that you need to support? What does your ideal client need to know or see from you?

Identify your key themes based on your four brand pillars, any dates, product or service launches, or deadlines first, and then check for other industry-wide events and activities that are taking place that you should be talking about, sharing, or joining in the conversation.

I suggest in the beginning creating one masterpiece of added value content per month and using the content model you will find in the downloadable workbook to help you repurpose it and break it down into lots of different supporting content throughout the month.

Once you have worked out what you will say, you can use some of the free tools available like Trello, Asana or CANVA to help you get organised, map out your posts and create fabulous visual graphics to accompany your content. I have added links to all these tools on my website www.iamlucyrennie.com.

Planning ahead will help keep you on track and produce more effective content and give you more time to allow your great ideas to come to life. And the best way to learn and improve? Block out some time to check out how the last quarter's content scored, which posts worked well and which not so well? Then plan in more of the good stuff for the next quarter!

The most important thing about creating your content is to make sure you have fun and enjoy yourself; being authentic and genuine is the best way to grow trust with your audience.

Disclaimer - there is a risk that by planning your content ahead of time in such a way, it becomes boring or less relevant. Make sure you are constantly checking in with your plan to ensure it is still up to date. Particularly in times of crisis, you need to make sure that you are mindful of events happening in the world or in your industry and that you don't miss the mark.

I believe that having a mix of planned and intentional content in line with your strategy and focus points in your business allows you to have the freedom to be able to create additional content on the go, such as in your stories or in your lives and gives you some time back to engage and join in conversations with other people online. It also means you can be super reactive when you need to be or jump on opportunities happening at that moment.

Just a note here about email marketing.

Make sure you focus on growing your email list. Do everything you can to create your own database and collect your ideal client's email addresses.

Of course, growing your audience on your different social media channels is important and will work towards building awareness for your brand and connecting with your audience. But remember that you don't actually own the data on those platforms. This means that if tomorrow Mark Zuckerburg or another decides either to cancel your account, start charging you for the privilege or suffer an outage and their platform goes down, you will not have any other way to reach, contact or communicate with your audience.

By starting to focus on building your own list, not only will this ensure that you own your own data, but it also means that you can positively communicate with your audience, nurturing them, and helping them to get to know you, like you and trust you.

You can add value through content, tips, or resources, let them know more about your brand, and encourage them to engage with and buy from you.

Email marketing is a very effective form of marketing, low cost, easy to manage, and gets results.

9

BECOMING THE BRAND THAT DOES

What if Beyonce, George Clooney or Brad Pitt wanted to do business with you? Would you treat them like any other client or customer? Of course not. You would fawn all over them.

 "Here is the Jedi Mind Trick to make you craved by your customers, envied by your competitors, and raved about in your industry: treat all customers like they are a celebrity,"[1]

INTERNATIONAL CUSTOMER SERVICE EXPERT GEOFF RAMM.

What would happen if you focused on creating such a mind-blowing experience and making your clients feel so good that they don't want it to end and keep coming back for more?

I am a massive believer in the power of people and how by creating a fantastic customer experience, you can make people feel special, show them you care and encourage them to come back time after time.

I remember going to our local pharmacy as a child with my mum when I was poorly to get some of that banana-flavoured yellow penicillin. Do you remember that stuff? It tasted so good! And as we walked in the lady behind the counter looked up at us and gave us the biggest smile, the cheeriest hello and asked us how we were doing. I must have only been about five or six years old, but do you know what? I can still remember how lovely it felt. I remember thinking, gosh, she recognises us, and she's pleased to see us, which made the whole experience special; I felt special.

Now, as it happens, I went on to work with Audrey, the pharmacy manager, from the age of fourteen until I went to university four years later, serving customers in the shop and helping behind the scenes, after school in the evenings and each Saturday.

I later learned that Audrey would welcome every single customer in the same friendly and warm way, as if they were her favourite customer, even when she had never met them before. It was Audrey who helped me to understand the power of absolute customer service, of making sure that everyone feels special, and I suppose, ultimately showing each person that engages with your business that you care every single time.

Audrey was my first mentor, a brilliant and fabulous business-woman who helped me grow and understand how important it is to value people and relationships.

It was with Audrey that I started to think about the "little things" that can make a big difference and develop trust and loyalty with your customers. It is something that I feel is important for all small businesses to think about, particularly in today's noisy and digital world where a lot of the time you don't get the chance even to meet your customers face to face.

Fixing that leaky bucket

If you know me or have heard me speak, you will know that I often talk about the concept of 'fixing your leaky bucket'.

A leaky bucket is simply a bucket with holes in it, which means that any water you pour into the bucket will start to leak through the holes. You can never completely fill your bucket to the top because there is always some water that is slipping away, so it becomes an endless cycle of topping up and slipping away, topping up and slipping away.

I often work with business owners who describe to me all the different things they are doing and all the time and money they are investing each month to attract new leads and clients to their business. They are proud to show me the latest trends, the fancy dashboards, and the complicated funnels they have in place.

And then, I ask them about their lifetime value and their customer retention strategy, and they suddenly go quiet.

 Customer lifetime value (CLV, or CLTV) is a metric that indicates the total revenue a business can reasonably expect from a single customer account throughout the business relationship.[2]

I want to invite you to think about your own business as the bucket and your clients as the water.

How leaky is your bucket?

I think it is easy in today's digital and fast-paced world to get caught up in the excitement of new marketing techniques, tools, and methods to attract and bring in new customers. There are a lot of marketing agencies and gurus out there who are teaching you how to bring in new clients, and it has become normal to constantly focus on new client acquisition and spend a lot of money in the process.

Now, don't get me wrong, I am not saying that you should stop trying to attract new clients to your business. In fact, for most of this book, that is what I am talking to you about and helping you to do.

However, I am encouraging you to think differently again at how you look at your sales and customer retention.

If you are delivering the best service and best quality products, if you are delighting your customers each and every time, then they will come back for more.

In leaky bucket terms, if you are doing everything right and your customer experience is five stars, then the number of holes in your bucket will be dramatically reduced, which in turn means that the amount of water or customers that slip away will also be reduced.

We know it is also easier to sell again to an existing client than to acquire a new one. Again, this makes total sense as you have already done all the hard work in building that goodwill and know, like and trust factors.

So, what if your strategy turned from a focus on acquiring new clients to focusing on delivering as much value as possible to keep hold of your existing ones?

In other words, what if you focused on customer retention and customer lifetime value?

For me, it seems logical that the most effective way to future-proof your business is to always offer 'Celebrity style service' to your customers so that not only do they keep coming back for more, but they also become your super fans and shout about you and your brand from the rooftops to all their friends and 600 connections!

Exercise: Celebrity service

Be honest for a moment with yourself and imagine that your favourite celebrity did indeed get in touch with you and wanted to work with you or buy your products or services.

- What would you do differently?
- Make a note of anything you think of in your downloadable workbook.
- If you have noted anything down, ask yourself why you are not doing those things already and what, if anything, is stopping you from implementing them today.

I believe that you should be able to create *Celebrity service* for every customer in your business, and I think the key driver to that is *Communication*. It is all about the way you communicate and manage people's expectations. It is about reducing the gap between what people expect from you and your brand and what you deliver. In other words, do you deliver on what you promise? Are you providing the service or quality that people expect from your brand?

The best way to achieve this in my opinion is to go above and beyond and add value every single time. I genuinely believe that it will never be a waste of time, money, or energy. You will always be building up your bank of goodwill.

This does not mean that things will not go wrong or mistakes will not be made, nobody is perfect, and brands should always be looking to evolve and grow, but how you deal with those mistakes will be the key to retaining your customers or not. And the pot of goodwill that you have been building up with them will go a long way to help this.

If you can demonstrate that you are a brand that genuinely cares about your customers and create a brand experience from A-Z that delights people at every step of the way, then I believe that you can create the magic, you can harness the power of the ripple effect.

The little things

Very often it is the little things that are not expected or are not absolutely "necessary" that surprise and delight people the most. It might be a welcome gift, a check-in, a personalised phone call or simply a thank you. You must decide what fits well with your brand and offering at the different stages of your customer experience.

———

Exercise:

- Take some time to map out your customer experience and different touch points and decide what your customers are expecting and when.
- Thinking about how you can communicate effectively with your customers at each journey stage is a great starting point.
- Why not include some moments to update them on progress or check in with them to ask for feedback?
- What little touches can you create to make your customers feel valued and cared for?
- How can you exceed their expectations and make them want to come back for more?

NB: Whatever you decide, ensure you are future-proofing it by embedding it into your business processes with a review loop.

10

WHAT IS GOOD COMMUNICATION?

Excellent and Effective communication is two-way.

It is about more than just broadcasting and exchanging information. It is about understanding the emotion and intentions behind the information. It is also about listening in a way that gains the whole meaning of what is being said so that each party can feel heard and understood.

Being able to communicate effectively is incredibly important to me and has been the key driver for most of my career, and I believe that if you can become a good communicator, then you have the power to change the world.

From working with both huge corporate organisations and hundreds of small businesses, I have witnessed the impact that both good and bad communication can have on customers and relationships, on employees and their engagement and ultimately on sales and brand reputation.

How you communicate enables you to create and develop a solid and inclusive brand and culture, engage with your clients and teams effectively, and allows you to grow trust and goodwill which impacts your reputation and, at the end of the day, your bottom line.

The way you communicate does have the potential to make or break your brand.

I wanted to share with you my thirteen points to consider and to help you to communicate more effectively as a brand and as a business owner and leader in your field:

1. **It starts with you.** It is your brand, your business and you get to decide how you want things to be. You set the tone, the standard, and the culture.
2. **Put yourself in other people's shoes.** Being able to see things from other people's perspectives and understand how they are feeling and what they need from you.
3. **Back to Basics**. Make sure you have the basics in place and a focus on managing expectations. What do people NEED to know? What do you NEED to know?
4. **Know your audience.** Remember that one size does not fit all. Once you have identified your key people, spend some time working out what is important to them, and what they care about and ask yourself why they should care about what you are saying or doing.
5. **Don't make assumptions.** Always remember to think about knowledge before assumptions. Sense check and ask yourself what the facts are. If you are not sure, then find out and check.

6. **Ask questions. It's not about you.** Open-ended questions and clean questions, be careful not to guide or orient people in your questions. People love to talk about themselves, so encourage them to do so and listen and learn.

7. **Authentic**. Be real. Don't try to be something you are not. The more authentic you can be, the more people will engage with you and connect with you. People want to get to know you, what you stand for and what you think.

8. **Be Vulnerable**. Don't be afraid to show your weaknesses or admit it when you don't know something or if you get something wrong or make a mistake. Remember it is how you deal with the problem or issue that matters. Don't be afraid to ask for help if you need it. People are more likely to engage with you if you show you are human.

9. **Listen to learn and be curious.** Stop listening to simply reply to people. Be intentional and really listen. Give people time to think, and notice the difference that makes to your relationship, the insights you will receive and the trust you can create.

10. **Language – Watch your language and tone**. Be mindful of the words you are using. Refer back to your tone of voice document. Avoid using jargon out of context and ensure you are aligned with your values and brand characteristics.

11. **Remember the little things.** Show you care. Say thank you and show appreciation and encouragement.

12. **Sense check.** Measure, review, update, learn, and test things. Remove if it's not working and repeat, repeat, repeat if it is.

13. **And yes it starts with you**. People are looking to you as the leader, the face behind your brand, to walk the talk, do what you say you're going to do, and lead by example. They will look to you for confidence and reassurance, particularly in times of uncertainty and crisis.

Finally, I wanted to share a last model that will help you reflect on how you communicate as a brand.

Thinking about the different ways your audience prefers to take in content and information is also a great way to help you connect with your key people and ensure that, no matter what the message, you can help them absorb the information in the most effective way for them.

The VARK model by Neil Fleming.

Visual - preferring information through graphs, diagrams, maps etc.

Aural - preferring to hear and listen to information such as audiobooks, podcasts, radio, lecture style, etc.

Read / Write - a preference for reading and writing such as manuals, reports, essays, and the internet.

Kinaesthetic - a preference for real things, such as demonstrations, and videos, and if it can be grasped, held, tasted, or felt.

Understanding and recognising these different styles and people's preferences can be life-changing for you as a small business owner, for your clients, your partners and teams and for your brand. It means that you can be super intentional about how you communicate and the tools and resources you need to create and implement.

So, for example, I have a solid Kinaesthetic learning preference, which means that I take in content, and I learn best through practical experiences, hands-on, case studies, real-life situations and a lot of trial and error. Because I'm aware of this, I can communicate this to someone trying to teach me something and save a lot of time and energy. But equally, I might be aware that one of my clients prefers more visual content, so I will prioritise more diagrams, graphs, or pictograms in my communication with them.

With this knowledge, you can adapt your communications and content to suit your audience. Or, as best practice when creating your content and communicating your brand messaging and pillars, make sure you have a thorough mix of the four different styles so that everyone can experience it in the best way for them.

PART 3

CONNECTION

11

WORD OF MOUTH

You have to start somewhere.

When I began my business seven years ago, back in 2015, I had to start from scratch. Although I had grown up on the edge of the Peak District and gone to school there, I had spent most of my professional life living and working in France and Luxembourg. And even when I moved back to the UK in 2009, I kept my job as Head of Communications, looking after more than 350 sites worldwide.

Every Monday morning, I would commute via the 6 am KLM flight from Manchester to Amsterdam Schiphol, and then on to somewhere around the world to visit one of the steel service centres I looked after and stay in yet another Hilton hotel. And if I wasn't travelling that particular week, I would work from my dining room table back home in Whaley Bridge.

Of course, I had friends and family here, I grew up and spent the first eighteen years of my life in the neighbouring village New Mills, but all my professional network was based around the world, anywhere but in Whaley Bridge in the High Peak, Derbyshire. This meant that when I made the huge decision to leave behind the corporate world and set up my own small business in 2014, I had zero network around me. In fact I thought I knew nobody.

I had no clients, associates, or community to lean on, support, or help me get going. (Apart from my husband and best friend, Paul Rennie, who could not have been more supportive and encouraging from the start, thank you).

I had to build my brand, reputation, and business from absolutely nothing, and I did it by using the power of word of mouth, by building relationships and rapport with my connections. This is the secret I want to share with you.

As you know, I am a huge believer in the fact that people do business with people and that for people to want to buy from you and engage with you, they need to get to know, like and trust you. And this can take a long time.

They have been there all the time, right under your nose!

Getting started is the biggest hurdle you must overcome when starting your small business. And really, what that means is making your first few sales. Because honestly, you don't have a business unless you are making money.

Whatever your business, whatever it is that you decide to sell, whether it be a product or a service, getting that first sale is a huge milestone for you and your business. It is your proof of concept, the proof that you have a viable business idea and one that people are willing to buy into. A product or service that people are willing to pay for.

How do you get past the first year?

I just want to say that it takes a lot more work and effort than people think to get your business off the ground. If you are reading this and are already making sales in your business, please take some time to acknowledge this and recognise your achievement.

This chapter will help you build on your success and hopefully encourage you to look at things differently and make things easier for you moving forward.

If you are reading this and have not yet made any sales in your business, I want to encourage you to keep going, and I hope that what I will share with you next will help you get over the first milestone and get started.

I am sharing this with you because it has always astounded me over the years when people tell me that they don't understand why something has not worked or why they have not made the sale when all they have done is sent one email, posted once or twice on their social media channel, or paid for an advert to run in a magazine. I have had many conversations with people who want to grow their business and are surprised when things don't work.

Therefore, I believe it is important that we all become champions for each other and support and encourage each other to keep going, deliver brilliant products and services and believe in ourselves. It is one of my most significant drivers for writing this book. It is my way of sharing as much as possible of my learnings with you to help you on your journey.

And because I genuinely believe in the power of word of mouth and creating trust and goodwill, and the real impact that this can have on your brand and in future-proofing your business, I'm on a mission to spread the word and show you what is possible.

Please stop being hard on yourself; it really does take so much more work, creativity, and grit than most people expect. It isn't easy, there is no quick fix, and if you want to do it well and sustainably, then it is a long game.

Twenty per cent of small businesses fail within the first year. By the end of the second year, thirty per cent of businesses will have failed. By the end of the fifth year, about half will have failed. [1]

How do you get started?

The one concept that most people seem to ignore or don't think about is the fact that you have the answer to your own marketing right under your nose.

You have to start with who you know, which means you need to begin with your own network and the people who already know, like and trust you.

When I launched my business back in 2015, I had no network, audience, or email list. Until that moment, nearly my whole career had been built outside of the UK, and here, I was launching a business from my dining room table in Whaley Bridge and looking to work with local small business owners, and I knew nobody who had their own business!

Or so I thought....

I realised that if I wanted to get some paying clients, then I needed to get myself out there. I needed to be visible, to let people know I was there and how I could help them. I needed to get in front of the right kind of people.

Although I had no idea where to start, what I did know was that people do business with people. I knew that if I could build a network of people who saw the value in what I was offering and liked me enough to trust that I would do a good job, I knew I had a good chance.

I sat down with Ellia, who was about eight months old, sleeping by my side, and I just googled everything to do with business networks, business associations and business directories in the High Peak and the Peak District. I got onto Google maps and created a thirty-mile radius around Whaley Bridge, and I realised that I was slap bang in the middle of some amazing cities and places like Manchester, Leeds, Sheffield, Derby, and Buxton.

Then I got a big piece of A3 paper and some felt tip pens and created my first mind map. I noted all the organisations I found that were linked to small business, like the Chamber of Commerce, Glossop Business ladies' network, the D2N2 Growth Hub, High Peak Network, High Peak Business Club, the FSB, Vision Buxton, WIBN.......

Exploring each one a bit further, I checked out the different events, the dates and the key people and made myself a bit of a plan.

Putting myself out there

The first event I ever attended was *Glossop Women's Network*. And I am honestly not exaggerating when I tell you that at the time, I thought it was the scariest thing I had ever done! Looking back now, of course, I can laugh about it, but at the time, I was absolutely petrified!

Not only was I getting out of the house for something "non-baby" related for the first time in about ten months, but it was also the first time that I was doing something for me, for my business, for my brand, and that changed the game for me.

It's funny isn't it, how our mind works! For the previous four-teen years, I had been used to travelling around the world, meeting with senior leaders and managers, and organising and hosting international events in places like Milan, Nice and Prague. It did not used to bother me when I had to stand up in front of a huge conference room full of key professionals from around the world and deliver a presentation to them. But there I was in the sleepy town of Glossop, in the heart of the Peak District, at the local cricket club absolutely terrified to stand up and tell my story to a group of about fifteen local busi-nesswomen.

I can remember physically shaking as I got up in front of them all to introduce myself, tell them a bit of my story, and share my new business venture. I joked about wearing high heels for the first time in ten months and how I had a baby sick on my shoulder. And then, slowly, seeing the other ladies smile back at me knowingly and nod along with me helped me to relax and feel more comfortable. I survived!

At that meeting, in June 2015, I met some brilliant business-women who I am still in touch with today and who have become great allies on my journey.

A special mention and thank you to Sharon Taylor from Paragon Print, Kelly Greenhalgh from Greenhalgh Accoun-tancy, Jo and Nancy Jaeger Booth from Social Media Makes Sense and Claire Bradshaw from Claire Bradshaw Coaching to name but a few.

That first network meeting was the catalyst and the springboard to building my business, growing my brand, and getting myself out there.

Do the free stuff

I know there are many people who might say differently and might not agree with this, and that is OK. But I genuinely believe that when you come from a place of really wanting to help others, when you want to make a difference, when you really want to add value, then I believe that delivering and creating free content and resources is one of the best ways to help you do that.

Firstly, because you are directly helping people, and secondly it is the best way for your audience, for your ideal clients to get to know you, to see how you work, to get a feel for what you are about and to engage with you.

They can get a taster and an introduction to see what it is like to work with you. And then, slowly but surely, they will start to like and trust you. They can learn from you, and by providing lots of free content, free resources, and free workshops, it means it is a low risk for them as well, which means that any barriers that could be in place are lower.

This was one of the first things I did. I realised the power of getting myself out there, in front of my ideal client, the kind of business owners I wanted to work with. I understood quickly that if I could just get in front of them, offer value, and help them even in the smallest way, then I could start to build relationships.

So, I delivered as many free workshops, presentations, and masterclasses as possible at as many different organisations from my list as possible. I shared free tools, resources, handouts and more with as many people as I could. (I continue to do this today through my free Facebook group *Communicate with Purpose*, weekly emails and all the free resources and templates that you can find on my website, including the downloadable workbook that accompanies this book).

Thanks to this strategy, I could get in front of business owners who needed to grow their businesses. They needed help to create their marketing and communications strategy, and I was getting in front of rooms full of these people. Ok, I might not have been paid, but the return on investment was tenfold because once I had written the presentations and created the slides, all I had to do was show up and deliver.

I was able to build relationships with the people within the networks and organisations, as well as the business owners who attended my workshops. And eventually, I began to get requests to deliver paid-for workshops, and that is when I knew everything was going to be ok; since then, I have never looked back. This was when it all started, the ripple effect that comes from word-of-mouth referrals and recommendations. I have built my six-figure business in the last seven years through word of mouth alone. Every client has come through via a referral or recommendation from one of my connections.

Do you hate networking and making small talk?

Yes, that's me! I'm super shy, I get nervous walking into a room full of strangers, and honestly, most of the time, I would rather curl up in a ball and hide away. However, I know there is no better way to build your business than through people and growing your network, so I force myself to do it. And do you know what, once you're in there and you have started the conversation you realise that it is never as bad as you thought it would be.

If this resonates with you, here are my six steps to make meeting and connecting with new people easier:

1. Remember it is not about you; it is about the person you are talking to.
2. Smile because nobody wants to speak to a grumpy person!
3. Ask lots of open questions and make them as specific and relevant as possible to the person you are talking to.
4. Be vulnerable and laugh away your nerves or the uncomfortable elephant in the room. Be honest and say, "I'm not good at this small talk thing, but I'd love to hear what you think about...."
5. Ask for help and advice.
6. Most importantly, be the one who actually LISTENS!

Investing in your own CRM

One tool that I recommend and one action that I recommend you start doing from today, if you don't already do so as you develop and grow your business, is to invest in your own CRM system.

A CRM system is a Customer Relationship Management system. In other words, it is a database where you can record essential information about your customers, potential customers and other key contacts. You could quite easily do this on an Excel spreadsheet, however, there are lots of really great ready-to-use CRM systems available out there that range in price depending on what you need it to do, from zero budget to huge budgets. I use Zoho CRM in my business and get the help and support I need from my wonderful clients and friends Sara, Chris and Ellie at JCM Business Solutions.

You should start as soon as possible in building your own CRM because your whole focus, I believe, should be on looking to grow and nurture your relationships. As you develop your network, grow your connections, and start to get to know all these people, you need to make sure that you are capturing the correct information and that you are using the information and managing everything in the most appropriate and the most effective way.

NB: Make sure you are in line with the latest **GDPR** (General Data Protection Regulations) guidelines about storing and using personal data.

To find out more about this you can visit: https://ico.org.uk

Some questions and details to find out to help you to build and nurture your relationships are:

- Where did you meet the person?
- What they are interested in,
- What other details do you know about them?
- Do they have children?
- When is their birthday?
- Where do they work?
- What is their business?
- What are they looking for?
- What are their challenges?
- Where do they need help?
- What have you talked about or discussed at previous meet-ups?

Find out everything that allows you to better help and support them and grow that relationship. Everybody's favourite subject is talking about themselves, so tap into that and ask questions, make it about them, and you will find that the conversation flows. All you have to do is listen. And then, make sure you capture everything in your CRM system to enable you to refer back to it time after time and add value where you can.

Making sales through the people you know.

We have looked at getting yourself out there and finding organisations and networks where your ideal clients hang out.

Now I want to encourage you to think entirely differently about your whole world and your own connections. By really embracing the true power of your connections and focusing your time and energy on those who already know, like and trust you.

Have you heard the saying "just six degrees of separation"?

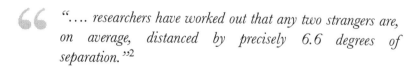 *".... researchers have worked out that any two strangers are, on average, distanced by precisely 6.6 degrees of separation."[2]*

This blows my mind. It is basically saying that we are only 6.6 connections away from every single person in the world. From the Queen, from Kate Moss or President Obama.

By simply shifting the way you look at things, identifying and understanding who your connections are, and looking at who currently makes up your own network, you can change the whole way you do business.

Remember that we said it takes, on average, eight touch points before someone trusts your brand enough to buy from you. And if you are starting out cold, trying to reach them across your social media channels or through advertising, then it will probably take you even longer.

How about instead of focusing uniquely on reaching your ideal clients, you focus instead on who already knows, likes, and trusts you?

Who are your family members? Brothers, sisters, cousins, nieces, nephews. Do they know what you do? Have you told them about your business? About your products and services? About your vision and what you have to offer?

These people have known you probably for years and will (in most cases) know you well, really like you and trust you too.

Who else do you know that will feel the same way about you?

Your best friends from school or university, your pals from the pub or the ones you play football with or go running with each week?

What about the mums and dads at the school gate?

How about your ex-colleagues from your previous role or maybe your first boss when you first started? Your bank manager or your next-door neighbours?

We naturally dismiss our relations and our existing connections because we think that because they are not our ideal clients, then they won't be interested, and therefore there is no reason to share your story with them.

Please change this way of thinking NOW and from today onwards. I want you to start to become strategic and intentional about building your own connections and using your network to grow your business and make more sales.

 "The average American knows about 600 people."[3]

If, on average, we each know 600 people, and each of your connections knows 600 people, that's 360,000. And they're right under your nose. And I could continue with each of their connections and their connections.

In other words, it's not necessarily your connections who are your ideal clients, but rather your connections' connections. By becoming intentional about your communication and sharing your story with the people you know, you can increase your reach and take advantage of more word of mouth, recommendations, and referrals. Remember, people buy from people and combine that with the TripAdvisor effect you will read about next, and I promise you can skyrocket your business.

On the tip of everyone's tongue

I want you to aim to be on the tip of everyone's tongue, at the forefront of their minds and become so good at telling people what you are doing and how you help people that nobody will forget you, and the referrals will come from far and wide.

- Do you know anyone who can help me with my marketing?
- Do you know anyone who can come and talk to my team about health and safety?
- Any ideas about what I could send to my customers this Christmas to say thanks?

Whatever your business, there will always be somebody asking a question that might be related to your brand, like those above. Someone looking for a recommendation or a referral, and the more of your connections that know about you, the more likely they are to talk about you or mention your name and brand.

Even if these people don't want to buy from you, they will be super happy to refer or recommend you. But remember, they can only do this if they know what you are doing, what you are selling and the types of clients you are looking for.

With this in mind, I want you to be intentional about how you communicate and ensure that your key people are kept up to date about your latest ventures and projects.

This next exercise will help you to do this and really start to identify your own connections map that you can build on as you grow.

———

Exercise: - Create your own *Connections map*

You will find an example of this and more information in your downloadable workbook.

- Find yourself a large sheet of white paper, minimum A3, but the bigger, the better and a pack of felt tip pens.
- Write your name in the middle of the paper and put a circle around it.

- Now you are going to create a mind map style diagram and capture as many of your different connections as possible, categorising them as you go.
- For example, close family, friends from school, friends from your football club, ex-colleagues, other parents from school, if you have a team, employees, suppliers, customers, or past customers.
- Once you have captured as many people as you can, start to think about them as your own personal cheerleaders.
- Have a look at each person or category and try and imagine the 600 connections they each have and the impact that this could have on your business.
- Finally, jot down some ideas in the table in the workbook about how you can make sure that all the people you have put down on your connections map know what you do, how you can help and how to find you. Keep in mind, that if they were to refer you or recommend you to one of their connections, what would they need to know to do it effectively?

———

12

EXPLORING OPPORTUNITIES

In the previous chapter, I talked to you about the power of word-of-mouth marketing and how impactful it can be on your business. You looked at identifying who those people are right under your nose, that already know you and trust you and who have the potential to refer you.

What you have started to do here is create your own stakeholder map for your business and brand. This is a key activity normally undertaken in the first stages of developing a communications strategy. We use it to identify all the different stakeholders or categories of people that should be included within the plan.

Stakeholder: a person with an interest or concern in something, especially a business.

I want to take this a step further with you now and help you expand on your map and then show you how you can use this tool differently.

I want to show you how you can develop and grow your brand through your connections and not just by encouraging people to recommend or refer you. I will make you a promise now because I am 100% convinced that by doing this next activity and following through on it, you will be able to transform the way you market and grow your business.

I promise you that by creating your own connections map and analysis and exploring the opportunities within it, you will be able to develop your own organic marketing strategy that will provide you with an endless amount of free promotional activity that you can undertake. Opportunities that I would classify as warm or very warm because you will be getting in front of new audiences and benefit from the transfer of good-will through association.

This is where the fun starts, and you can be as creative as you want to be.

It all comes down to creating "win-win" relationships and collaborations. And, of course, it goes without saying that everything comes from a place of integrity and transparency.

———

Exercise:

Find that big sheet of A3 paper with your mind map on it.

Here is a list of different stakeholder categories that I want you to think about as you build on your mind map.

Close family, friends from school, friends from the football club, ex-colleagues, other parents from school, if you have a team, employees, suppliers, customers, past customers,

Bank manager, your trade body if you have one, your local Chamber of Commerce, quality assurance company, HMRC, local journalists, publications, the BBC, and specific industry publications. Local schools, colleges, and universities.

I want you to think about all your different stakeholders, people and organisations that might have an interest in your business or vice versa and note them down on your map.

The final category of people I want you to think about and remember you don't have to share this with anybody is to think about your *'Super fans'*.

Your *Super fans* are those people who just think you are brilliant. No matter what you do, they think you are the dog's dinner. They love what you do, they love how you talk, they love how you show up, and they love your products or services. In other words they think you are terrific and importantly they trust you 100%.

They might be people who have been previous customers or existing customers. They might be friends, family, an old teacher, an ex-boss, or a colleague. These are the people that I want you to nurture; these are the people who are already shouting about you from the rooftops. You need to make sure that these people know exactly what you are doing, what you are selling and what you are offering so that when they are recommending you, they are doing it the right way.

Find the table in the downloadable workbook that looks like the image below.

1) Name / Category	2) What is important to them?	3) How could you help them?	4) How could they help you?	5) Score	6) Ideas
Your Support Team / Trusted partner (they are my bookkeepers)	Looking to grow their business in the creative sector	Introductions Workshop in FB group and the Future-Proof Club	Get in front of their clients by delivering a workshop	10 / 10	Case study Joint event Sponsor my retreat Testimonials

I am going to take you through how you carry out an analysis of each of your connections or stakeholders. It is worth noting that this is a great tool to help you work through other challenges or areas of your business as it helps you look at many different situations and see things from other people's perspectives.

 "You never really understand a person until you consider things from his point of view.... Until you climb into his skin and walk around in it."

HARPER LEE, TO KILL A MOCKINGBIRD.

Take each category one at a time and insert them into the spreadsheet. Ideally, you will have a specific line for each individual stakeholder; however if you have lots of people, it makes sense to start at the category level first.

I will walk you through the example found in the table, which is using one of my key stakeholders, *Your Support Team Ltd*, a bookkeeping business owned by my wonderful friends and clients, Hayley and Claire.

1) Column 1 - Name / Category

This step is easy and requires no explanation from me.

2) Column 2 - What is important to them?

Here I want you to think about what is important to them. I know that *Your Support Team* are looking to grow their business. I know that they are looking to work with larger organisations or bigger small businesses in the creative sector.

So, I'm going to add that detail into column two.

3) Column 3 - How could you help them?

If you know their objective, I want you to think about how you could help them achieve that goal.

In this example, I could introduce them to some of my other key partners who work in that particular sector, or I could invite someone from their team to come and deliver a workshop to members of my Facebook community *Communicate with Purpose* or my membership, the *Future-Proof Club.*

In that way, I'm helping them to get in front of new audiences very similar to their ideal client base and simultaneously deliver value to my members. They can demonstrate that they are experts in their field and maybe give a free resource to my members to encourage them to sign up and join their mailing list.

I am also a client of theirs, so I could be part of a case study with them or invite them to sponsor one of my strategic retreats.

There are lots and lots of different examples of how I could help them to grow their business. The key here is to capture as many ideas as possible and return to them when you need inspiration.

4) Column 4 - How can they help you?

It is essential to think about how they can help you because don't forget that what we are trying to do here is to create a bank of win-win relationships and collaborations.

With Your Support Team in mind, they work with hundreds of small businesses that are all 99.9% my ideal clients. So, if I can get in front of some of these clients and deliver a workshop, add value, demonstrate my expertise, and show them how I can help, that would really help me grow my client portfolio.

The best thing about this kind of collaboration is that you go in front of these new audiences already recommended.

By inviting me in to speak to their clients, *Your Support Team* are demonstrating that they think highly of me, which gives me credibility and makes it easier for me to earn their clients' trust and buy-in.

5) Column 5 - Score

Here I want you to give each stakeholder a score out of ten, ten being very high and one being very low. Because not all your connections can offer opportunities that will deliver as much impact as others, it is important to score each one on the potential impact this collaboration might have on your business.

This will evolve and change in time as you build relationships, as your connections grow, and as your business evolves. However, by giving each one a score today, you will be able to filter and prioritise the opportunities and formulate your roadmap for the next twelve months.

6) Column 6 - Ideas

This is the final column, and it's a space where you can capture any ideas you have at this time. Be creative and think out of the box. You don't have to share this with anybody. It is just for you to think of ideas and how you can leverage your connections to support your business.

Put down any ideas that you have, no matter how wacky they are, no idea is a bad idea. Some suggestions from me could be speaking as a guest on a podcast, creating case studies, testimonials, guest blog writing, interviews, sponsorship deals, partnerships, events, workshops, masterclasses, worksheets, quizzes, affiliate schemes, a day in the life of…, newsletters, trade shows.

The list is endless, and you will always come up with new ideas, so keep your connections map and spreadsheet close to hand.

Your done for you communications plan.

A great tip is that every time you have something you want to communicate with people, something you want to share like a new product or service launch, or some special news, get out your connections map and tools, and work your way through the list.

You could even use this for your regular content planning and communications roadmap.

Take each stakeholder into consideration and think about each one in terms of what they need to know and why, how they can help you and how and when you should communicate with them. Are there specific channels or formats that would be more effective?

How can you measure your effort and see what is working and what isn't?

And then identify what you can learn from this each time. Remember to scrap the things that don't work well and aren't effective and repeat the things that do work well and get results.

NB: There is a communications plan template in the downloadable workbook.

13

THE TRIPADVISOR EFFECT

The way we interact with brands and businesses has changed. I believe that for you as a small business owner, the game has changed, and in a good way.

The way we interact with each other and our favourite brands has been transformed thanks to the internet and the different social media platforms. There are no longer any barriers due to travel, language, or money; we can reach and communicate with pretty much who we like, how we like and where we like.

This means that for you, as a small business owner, the world is your oyster.

You don't even need to have a website today.

The same can be said for how we interact and engage with brands and businesses and what we expect from them.

It's no longer enough just to create an advertising campaign to promote your new product or service. People are consuming content in different ways, they want different things, they want you to be present in different places and they want you to be consistent everywhere you go.

Think about how you go about finding a new restaurant, a new hairdresser or even a new fridge or washing machine.

In the past, you would probably have made your decision based upon the best advert, a promotional discount or because your favourite celebrity endorsed it. And, of course, these things do still come into play, I'm not dismissing them.

However, think about what you do today when you buy something new, or you're looking for a new restaurant to try. Your instinct is to ask your friends, colleagues or family for a recommendation and then before you buy or book, you go to the reviews section to check out what other people have said about it.

People no longer take what brands tell them about their products and services as truth. The best way for them to know if a product or service will be right for them is to see and hear what people like them think. They want to know about other people's experiences and how they rate the brand.

People trust people like you and me to give an honest review more than they trust the brands themselves. This has changed the world we live and work in.

This is what I call the *TripAdvisor effect*, and I think it is the most exciting thing you can embrace for your small business.

Why?

Because no matter how small you are or what little budget you have, you can play in the same league as the big boys, and you can make a massive difference to your brand, your reputation and ultimately, your business and bottom line.

How?

By simply doing what you do best. By looking after your customers time after time and providing them with an outstanding experience that they don't forget, they won't want to leave.

Every small business like yours now has the opportunity to stand out from the crowd, play amongst the big boys, and grow by delighting people and encouraging them to talk about you and your business.

 "People are four times more likely to buy from you when they've been referred by a friend."[1]

This statistic blows my mind. It blows my mind for lots of reasons, and I think the main reason is just what a tremendous opportunity this is and how exciting it is. This, for me is the true essence of genuine, honest marketing. It's growing your business through word-of-mouth; it's growing and building your business by simply doing a good job and doing what you say you're going to do.

When people are happy with your product or service, they are more than happy to recommend and refer you. And when they are really happy, they want to shout about you from the rooftops and tell everyone they know about you.

How amazing is that? And I just don't think some small business owners take this seriously. I don't think they realise the true potential of this opportunity. To create a ripple effect.

"92% of people trust recommendations from people they know."[2]

That's huge.

This means that if someone recommends your business to someone else, then 92% of the time that new person will trust the recommendation enough to buy from you.

And it only gets better as we analyse the impact referrals and recommendations can have on your average client Lifetime value.

Lifetime value means the total amount somebody invests in your business from the start of their journey with you to the end.

The lifetime value for a referral, a new customer that you get through a referral, is 16% higher than that of a new customer who comes directly to you and has not been referred in.

This means that people are more likely to buy from you when they've been referred to you by someone they know, but they're also more likely to stay longer and buy more from you. 16% more in fact than someone who comes to you directly.

In the B2B (Business to Business) world, so for those selling a product or service to another business, we know that 84% of decision-makers start their buying process through a referral. In other words, they ask for a recommendation or a referral first. Before they go to Google, before they do any further research, the first thing they do is ask people they know who they would recommend. Who would they go to for that particular type of product or service?

I can't find the words to express how passionate I am about this and how important I think it is for you and your small business. If there is one thing you are going to do tomorrow in your business to grow it, attract more of the right people and make it sustainable and Future-Proof it, I want you to really embrace *the TripAdvisor effect.*

I would love you to become intentional about how you can grow and nurture your own bank of cheerleaders.

This is what I encourage all of my clients to do, and I would love for you to make this your primary focus too. To make it your mission to build a bank of people, customers, superfans who love what you do, who think that you are brilliant and who keep coming back for more.

People who want to help you and are happy to recommend and talk about you.

They are happy to do this because they have found the secret. They have found the thing that works and want to share it with the world, and they will do that.

You know that excited feeling.... when you have found a new restaurant that's simply amazing, or you've had brilliant service from a new business manager or a new product. You want to talk about it and tell everyone about it because you're so excited and you can't get enough of it.

That's what I want you to embrace, to be intentional about, to be really purposeful about.

 "83% of consumers are willing to refer after a positive experience, yet only 29% actually do."[3]

So, what does that mean? That means that 83% of your customers are happy to make a referral, write a recommendation, give you a testimonial and help you with a case study. Still, in reality, only 29% of them do.

That's a fifty per cent gap. A massive, missed opportunity. You have got all these people who want to shout about you and who want to share their love for your business, and you are not giving them an opportunity to do it.

Maybe you're not asking them at all, or perhaps you're not reminding them or giving a gentle nudge?

———

Exercise: Review your reviews

Take some time now to consider how these statistics apply to your business.

- How often do you invite people to give you feedback or leave a review?
- How often do you encourage your existing customers to refer you to a friend or colleague?
- What systems do you have to capture feedback, reviews, and referrals?

———

Treat reviews like gold dust.

I believe you should treat reviews like gold dust because they are the essence of your sustainable marketing plan. Because you know that you are delivering outstanding service and being the best at what you do, it should not be difficult for you to receive great feedback and reviews.

By being strategic about collecting and sharing reviews from your customers, you will be able to tap into the magic that happens through the power of referrals.

Why? Because people want to see and hear from other people about their experience with you and your product or service, so by sharing your reviews, you're providing them with proof that what you are doing is of value.

And the more reviews you have that tell a story, show emotion, and resonate with your potential customers, the more likely they will like what they see and feel confident enough to trust you and buy from you.

How to get five-star reviews every time

What can you do to encourage people to spend a few minutes and leave you a review?

One of the main reasons I hear my clients share about why they don't get as many reviews as they should is because it makes them feel icky and a bit queasy reaching out to ask people to leave a review. So, they don't!

What do you think? When was the last time you asked somebody to leave you a review?

Put yourself in your customers' shoes again. Let's think about it from your experience when you are pleased with a product or service.

Do you ever think, "oh gosh, no way, how cheeky of them or how rude of them to ask me for a review"? Or do you think more along the lines of, "yeah, I'd be thrilled to write a review because I'm pleased with the experience and the high standard of service?"

If you're being honest with yourself, I bet you know that you are part of that 50% gap. You are up for leaving a glowing review, you are motivated for it, happy to do it, but then forget about it, you get distracted, and you miss the moment.

Or maybe the process was too complicated or too fiddly? Perhaps you were asked to log in to a particular site or account, and it just became too much like hard work?

What if it was made as easy as possible for you to leave your review? If you were invited to leave a review at the right moment when you were buzzing because you were super happy with the results you got from the product or the service, or you were delighted with your stay in that holiday cottage.

Nine times out of ten, I think you would do it. So, it's not about your customers not wanting to do it; it's more about making sure you provide the path of least resistance when you invite people to do it.

———

Exercise:

- What can you do differently in your business to capture as many reviews as possible?
- How can you make it as easy as possible for your customers to leave you a review?
- What can you do to ensure that you don't feel icky or queasy about asking customers to leave a review?

———

The simplest and most effective way to achieve this is to normalise it. To embed it within your internal processes and within your customer journey. Those of you who have a more formal system in place in your business, maybe a quality management system like an ISO certification, will know that getting feedback from your clients and customers is essential.

You need to get quality testimonials from your clients that demonstrate that you are doing what you say you are going to do.

When it becomes a part of your everyday business process, I believe it takes away the ickiness and that craziness because you are doing it from a place of genuine care and to continuously improve and develop your product or service.

Make it about your customer and take the emphasis off you as a business owner. If you make it about how you want to evaluate your products and service and how you want to get feedback, then I believe that that also helps to take the pressure off things. Although, of course, you may still have that icky feeling if you know deep down that you are not providing good value and excellent service. In that case, I wouldn't be comfortable asking for reviews and feedback either!

The best time to ask

The most optimum time to invite people to give feedback is when they get the results they want and when they're pleased with your products or service.

This will differ depending on your type of business. It might be whilst your customers are still in your shop or on your business premises, so before they leave, you might ask,

"Could I take five minutes to ask you a few questions about your experience with us today?"

Or it might be that at the end of the day, at that point in the journey. You might email them with a link to some questions or ask them to leave a review.

This could be reinforced with a personalised phone call, voice message or a little video that allows you to be personal, with some warm outreach.

Face to face, when they are with you, give them a card to fill in whilst they are still in your reception area and invite them to pop it into a box to be entered into a prize draw.

Send them an email afterwards with a link to the questionnaire, or why not send them a handwritten postcard to say thanks with a QR code on the back to access the survey and a reward?

I think this also leads me to a really important point: showing up and being real, vulnerable, and honest. Letting your customers know that leaving you a review can make a massive difference to you and your business. Share with them the value and impact that they can provide by taking just a few minutes out of their day to do that for you. Be you, be natural and be honest, explain that you'd love to get some more reviews to let people know about how you work and how you can help. Let them know the impact excellent reviews can have on your business.

I believe that if we can be authentic in that sense, then it helps us to connect with our customers, and they can get a real inkling about what's important to us. And if they can see how important it is for you and your business, then I believe they will be much more likely to go ahead and leave their review.

The survey itself

Make the survey super accessible, easy to navigate and keep your questions to a minimum.

Where is the best place to collect reviews?

Start simple

You could choose to create your own on a simple spreadsheet or printed card or go one step further and create a simple Google form, Zoho survey or Survey Monkey.

Create your own simple questionnaire that people can fill in and don't forget to leave a space at the end inviting them to leave a comment or a review.

NB. You can find a free downloadable template to create your own Google form to help you get started with this on my website.

There are many other places where people can leave reviews, which will differ depending on the type of business you have, the kind of product or service you have, and the industry you work in. There is no right or wrong answer to this, so I recommend you do your own research and find the best place for your business to encourage people to go and leave them a review.

However, I do recommend that you focus on one specific place in the beginning. Choose one platform and then drive people to that place because if you give people too much of a choice and too many options, they lose momentum. Because they don't know which to choose or don't want to make that decision, they are much more likely not to decide and not leave a review.

The first place to look at would be Google reviews. This is advantageous for many reasons, the first reason is that Google is the biggest search engine in the world, so any reviews left on its own platform are more likely to be privileged than elsewhere. This works well for brick-and-mortar businesses, for products and if and when you are using your Google My Business profile. Having your reviews pop up when someone searches for you in the Google bar is perfect.

Depending on where your ideal client hangs out, you might prefer to go with one of the social media channels' platforms, where you can also invite your customers to leave you a review. For example, that might be on your Facebook page, or it might be on your LinkedIn profile, where people can leave you a review or a testimonial.

The Top 5 review consumer and business review websites are:

1. **Google my business** - Did you know that Google's search engine performs over 3.5 billion searches per day

2. **Amazon** - Amazon is much more than book reviews; average monthly US traffic (Alexa): 85.44 million

3. **Facebook** - Since most users on the site already have a Facebook account, the process of leaving a business review is relatively friction-less

4. **Yelp** - Yelp has become a name synonymous with business reviews, as the site has over 102 million reviews and counting.

5. **TripAdvisor** - TripAdvisor operates websites internationally in over 25 countries.

https://www.vendasta.com/blog/top-10-customer-review-websites/

Don't forget that if you're selling a product through other retailers, then they will be able to collect and manage reviews for you too. Think John Lewis, Argos, or Etsy.

It doesn't stop there!

The work doesn't stop here; this is just the beginning. Once you have collected your review, now is the time for you to leverage and maximise its power.

This is where the concept of social proof comes in. I strongly encourage you to incorporate these testimonials and reviews into your content and communications plans.

People want to see and hear from other people about their experience with you and your brand, so by sharing your reviews; you're providing them with proof that what you are doing is of value. And the more they like what they see or hear, the more likely they will buy from you.

CONCLUSION - THE RIPPLE EFFECT

 "A little magic can take you a long way!"

ROALD DAHL

Clarity, Communication and Connection are the *three clear steps to Future-Proof your business,* and the ripple effect of this is where I believe the magic happens.

You have clarity about who you are as an entrepreneur, about what your small business is about, and you know what makes you unique. You are clear about why people should choose you and why people should work with your brand, and you know how you can help people.

You also know who you can help, the kind of people you want to attract to your business and the situations where you can make a real difference and achieve wonderful results for your clients.

You have worked out the best way to tell your story, communicate what it is you do, share your message in the best way, and nurture those people who engage with you, buy from you and work with you.

You have learned the importance of building relationships, of fixing your leaky bucket, and you have your own connections map and plan to help you reach out, build awareness for your brand and connect with people in a win-win and sustainable way.

Now that you have got these three pieces of the puzzle in place, I believe that there is no stopping you. There is nothing stopping you from growing a fantastic business that people love and trust.

There is no better way to *Future-Proof* your business than to create a business that feels good, works for you, and that you can fall in love with time after time.

I want you to have absolute confidence in your products and service, in your customer service and in the experience that your people have with your brand.

I want you to be able to manage the expectations of your clients so much so that because you nurture them and delight them at every step of the way, they don't want to leave.

And so, they become your cheerleaders. People who just love what you do. Who shout about you from the rooftops, refer you to their family and friends, and keep coming back for more!

This is the ripple effect. This is the MAGIC!

In nearly thirty years of working with small businesses and twenty-five years' experience in communications, marketing, and business strategy, I think this is the most important lesson that I have come to learn and understand, and I have made it my mission today to share this with as many small business owners as I can.

It is giving me goose pimples as I write this and think about and choose the words I want to use and share with you.

I truly believe that THE most effective, the most sustainable, the most authentic, and the most natural, wholesome and fulfilling way to grow, build and future-proof your business is by embracing the power of word-of-mouth.

As Alex Hormozi describes, *"Marketing is there as a replacement to 'Word-of-Mouth'."*

In other words, businesses only need to engage in marketing activity to fill the gap that exists because they don't have enough word-of-mouth, goodwill, and social capital.

This means that the more you deliver value, the more people will come back for more and the more they will encourage and create word-of-mouth recommendations and referrals, the less you will need to rely on other marketing methods.

The more you fix your leaky bucket, the more sustainable your business becomes.

And the final piece of the puzzle is that now you have got your own connections map, your own holistic and authentic win-win marketing plan where you can support other business owners within your circle of trust. You can create a broader and bigger impact on the wider community while promoting your own business by getting in front of new audiences and growing awareness of what you do and the value you offer.

Ok, I can hear you smiling and asking me if that means that once you have done all this can you go and sit in the Bahamas on a sun lounger drinking piña colada all day?

Ha ha, I'm afraid not, but that's not the point of why we are doing this anyway, is it?

We are doing this for the love of our small business and because we love what we do.

Because we love it so much and because we have uncovered the magic, it doesn't feel like work at all, does it?

So, I'm afraid this is not the end.

I think it is just the beginning. This is where the hard work starts, because as your business grows, you are learning, and you are making mistakes. You are finding your feet and testing out new ideas, you're building your audience and delivering more and more value.

The challenge you have moving forward, the real question of how-to future-proof your business is how you can make sure that you can maintain those high standards as you grow, as you build a team and as your business evolves.

It is making sure that your reviews are consistently five stars. It is remembering why you are doing what you are doing and ensuring that any decisions and actions you take align with your purpose and values.

And so, as you grow, as you see the success that you deserve because of the great job you're doing, you'll be confronted with new challenges. These might be taking on new people and building a team, in which case your biggest challenge is going to be how to maintain your vision and your values.

You'll need to think about creating a culture that's in line with where you want your business to be. And how to make sure that you can keep consistency in everything you do and everywhere you are?

Managing people is one of the hardest things in the world and is one of the primary reasons why businesses go wrong.

You may face challenges of how to increase capacity, serve more people and maintain the same levels of quality, customer service and the personal touch that you've been so renowned for.

For me, these aren't problems to worry about; these are new adventures that you can have fun exploring.

I think what is important is to keep coming back to these three steps and your brand foundations.

Remember why you are doing what you are doing. Being able to remind yourself of why you started this journey and to make sure that you are checking in with yourself regularly, to not only acknowledge your monumental achievements up to this point, but also to make sure that you are still on track, and you have not forgotten what is important to you.

As Paul Jarvis said in his book The Company of One - "better doesn't have to be bigger".

As we come to the end of this journey together, my final task is for you to set up a simple roadmap and dashboard that allows you to step back and lift your head out of your business at least once every quarter.

That encourages you to check in with your vision and goals, review how things are going, and ask yourself how you can improve and do better.

I invite you to ask lots of questions, to be curious as to why something is like it is or how you can improve it and then to listen and take on board the answers.

Make sure that you have **Clarity** and that you are intentional about what you are doing and why.

Ensure that you have a clear and effective **Communication** plan in place that starts with you and that emanates from inside your business, exceeding the expectations of your clients, your team, and all other key stakeholders.

And that you focus on **Connection**, building your word-of-mouth capital, harnessing the power of the TripAdvisor effect, and growing and nurturing your superfans and connections.

This is the key to the *Ripple Effect* **and Future-Proofing** your business; this is how you can ensure the magic continues to sparkle.

EPILOGUE - THE GOLDEN GOOSE

I could not write this book about the love of small business without talking to you about the Golden Goose.

This is a concept that has only taken me forty-four years to accept, acknowledge and embrace finally and I now believe fundamentally that this is one of the most important things that any small business owner and entrepreneur need to understand and recognise.

You need to put your own oxygen mask on first.

Do you know I used to travel on at least two aeroplanes every week for more than five years and when the air stewards would tell us to put our own oxygen mask on first before helping others, I never understood why! But now I know it makes complete sense.

If you remember the story of the Golden Goose, the fairy-tale. It's about a special golden goose that kept laying magical golden eggs. Obviously, the farmer was delighted because he was very poor and needed the money and the golden eggs were his way to fortune, providing supplies, riches, and wealth for him and his family.

The goose would lay one golden egg each day. But the farmer was greedy and wanted more. He became impatient and killed the goose to open its tummy and get more of the golden eggs. Of course, when he opened the goose, there were no more eggs inside.

The moral of the story is that not only did he not find the golden eggs that he was looking for, but he also killed the source of the wealth that was providing for himself and his family.

Denise Duffield Thomas talked about this metaphor in her book Chillpreneur and it hit home for me.

> *"You are the Golden Goose. Without you - you lose the essence of your business. Your energy deserves to be protected."*
>
> DENISE DUFFIELD THOMAS

It is the same for you as a small business owner, you must consider yourself the Golden Goose and protect yourself at all times. Because if you are not in a good place, if you are not looking after yourself, and you are not prioritising your well-being then you are not going to be able to do what you need to do.

If you are not in a good place and able to enjoy your business, then you will not be able to show up in the right way as your true self. The impact of this on your business and the people you want to support and look after will be huge.

I suppose my message to you here is to take the time to get to know yourself.

Get to know who you are and how you work. Find out what it is that you are doing when you are feeling good and what it is that you are doing that does not make you feel good.

Become good at recognising when you are feeling a bit low on energy and notice what that looks and feels like. What signs do you need to look out for that tell you that you're running low or you need some time out?

What do you need to do to ensure you can protect yourself, you, the Golden Goose?

Get clear on your boundaries.

I believe one of the best ways to look after yourself and make sure you can put on your oxygen mask guilt-free, is to think about your boundaries, what you say yes to and what you say no to.

A great way to look at this is to make a list of what I call non-negotiables.

———

Exercise:

Find yourself a notebook and pen (or find the section in the downloadable workbook) and write a list of all the things that are important to you.

- What are your priorities?

- What are the things you need to do or put in place to show up as the best version of yourself? For example, I know that to be in a good place, I need to exercise daily, drink lots of water, eat healthily and get at least 8 hours of sleep.
- What are the things that you need to do?
- Make a list of things you don't want to do anymore.
- Maybe it is a certain type of person that you don't want to work with.
- Maybe it is that you don't want to work in the evening. Or perhaps you don't want to deliver a particular workshop or provide a specific product anymore.

Whatever your non-negotiables might be, write them down. Make a list of the things you DO want.

- Maybe you want to be paid a specific price, in advance or simply on time.
- Or is it important for you to work with people who do what they say they are going to do?
- Maybe you know you need to surround yourself with the right kind of people. Is that joining a mastermind or another group of business owners?
- Maybe it's about dedicating more time to spend with your partner or children.

———

There are no right or wrong answers to this exercise. The key is to take a moment to sit with yourself and recognise what it is that you want deep down. Once you understand this, you can put things in place to help you to look after yourself and to protect the Golden Goose.

As I talked about at the beginning of this book. I believe that as a small business owner, the keys to success are all based around mindset. You can be as gifted and talented as you want, but if you don't have the right mindset and the resilience, grit and drive to keep yourself going when you're on that rollercoaster ride, then I think you're going to find it hard.

These are things that you can work on. These are things that you can explore, grow, and develop, and it starts by recognising the stories that are taking place in your mind. By noticing the way you approach things, and the way things make you feel.

There are so many books, resources, tools and excellent coaches and mentors out there for you to learn from that I highly recommend you get started if you haven't already.

And you'll find that as your business reaches a new level or as you reach a new stage in your journey or a new challenge, new mindset gremlins will always appear to challenge you.

As Henry Ford said, *"What got you here, won't get you there."*

And this is true for your life as a small business owner and your mindset. Just when you think that you have solved your limiting beliefs or a particular mindset issue, another one comes along.

As you reach new levels, you will discover new mindset challenges to unpick and explore, and I don't think that will ever end; I think it's inevitable. That's part of the rollercoaster ride.

I believe this journey of self-development is all part of being a human being. It's what keeps you alive and is part of the joy, satisfaction, and reward of doing what you do. Creating and growing a business that you love, that you can be proud of and that you know is making a bigger impact in the world.

In 2022, it's also about how you want to feel, ensuring you can embrace being in the present and enjoy the journey, even more than simply celebrating the outcomes.

I think that spending the last two years surviving a global pandemic has encouraged us all to rethink what is important, to take stock and look at where we are and ultimately question what we're trying to achieve, why we do what we do and how we want our lives to be.

When I listen to what you are saying and think about the conversations we have been having, it seems that you all agree that you don't want to be caught up in a crazy whirlwind anymore of non-stop busyness and overwhelm.

You want to feel more in control of what you are doing, where you spend your time and energy, and, of course, have a real understanding of why you are doing it.

And to do this, you have to make some choices.

You simply cannot do everything, and you will find that as your business grows and you grow, there will be certain things that are no longer relevant to you or appropriate.

Maybe they become less of a challenge, or they don't excite you as much as they used to do.

Or maybe you will develop new programmes, new products or services or ways of doing things for new audiences that mean your heart is in a different place.

And maybe, spending time with your family and friends at the weekend (or having a sneaky Sunday snooze) instead of being distracted by your phone or laptop is more important to you now.

As Sean Covey describes: *"Saying YES to one thing means saying NO to another."*

I think this sums it up really, it can be super hard to say NO to certain things, for many reasons. We don't want to let people down, we have always done it, or we want to help or support someone. (I'm sure there are lots of other reasons too!)

But if you flip it, reframe it, and think of it differently, it can make more sense and help you take back control. Learning to say NO more often and privileging those things that are important to you is probably one of the hardest and most impactful things you can do as a small business owner.

Protecting your time, priorities and energy allows you to hone in on what's important to you. You can then decide how you really want to spend your time and what you focus on, enabling you to move forward in the right way for you.

And don't forget, you can still be a "nice" person and say no too!

One task I advise my clients to do is to prepare some key phrases or even email or text templates that you can have ready to use when you want to say no. That way, you're not put on the spot, and you can reply confidently but kindly.

Remember, if you get stuck in the moment, buy some time, thank them, and tell them that you will come back to them in the next day or two.

And if you are still unsure what you should be saying YES or NO to, then why not create a list of things that bring you joy, that make you happy and feel energised and a list of things that don't? And then see what comes up for you....

As we reach the end of this book, I'd like to take a minute to thank you for sticking with me to the end.

I really hope you've enjoyed it and that you've found some of the activities and suggestions useful and I can't wait to hear how you get on.

Remember to find the joy in what you do, be yourself and keep showing up and I promise it will make the biggest difference.

I would absolutely love to hear from you if you have any questions, or feedback or maybe you have some stories that you'd like to share with me.

Please do reach out at lucy@lrcomms.co.uk or on Instagram at @iamlucyrennie

Have fun,

Lucy x

WAYS TO WORK WITH ME

Join me in my membership - The Future-Proof Club

A safe space and community for small business owners like you who are looking for strategic help and accountability in growing your business, creating a great brand and attracting more of the right kind of clients.

- Weekly check-ins
- Monthly training workshops
- Monthly planning and accountability workshops
- Guest experts
- Private Facebook group
- Online portal full of valuable resources and training

https://go.lrcomms.co.uk/future-proof-club

My Mastermind programme

If you're a small business owner, working on your own and looking for support, guidance and fun, then this 11-month programme is for you.

- Monthly 121 sessions
- Weekly check-ins on a particular theme or topic
- Monthly spotlight sessions where each member will have the hot seat to discuss, brainstorm or ask for support on a particular topic.
- Quarterly planning workshops to map out your strategy and roadmap
- Private WhatsApp group.

And my new online portal for replays, resources and other tools.

https://go.lrcomms.co.uk/mastermind-waitlist

121 Mentoring Programme

Are you considering taking on a marketing communications apprentice, but lack the time to mentor them yourself? Or perhaps you have a member of staff who lacks the experience and needs some expert guidance to help them grow in their role?

My mentoring programme offers support, guidance and advice both to you as the business owner and your in-house marketer. It gives you the certainty that you are building expertise in-house and peace of mind that everything is under control as you do that.

https://lrcomms.co.uk/my-mentoring-programme/

121 Strategy programmes and workshops

My 1-2-1 Strategy Sessions allow you to tap into my support and expertise, helping you develop your brand and business in a way that works and feels good for you.

We schedule time to discuss your business in a safe and confidential environment. Depending on what you want to explore, we could set aside an hour as a one-off, a half day, a full day or a series of sessions.

We'll look at what you're doing, and why you're doing it and create the strategy and roadmap together to help you to achieve your goal.

https://lrcomms.co.uk/my-121strategysessions/

WHAT PEOPLE SAY ABOUT ME

"Working with Lucy has been transformational, not only for my business but also for the way I approach it and feel about it. Lucy's passion, knowledge and ability to understand you so well means that she helps me to implement the right things and hold off those that are less important.

Lucy's ability to bring joy to the processes mean that I've tackled things I have always steered clear of and have begun to look at growing beyond my original desires because it now feels achievable and more than that – fun!

The way that Lucy brings people together means that I now feel that whilst I am a sole trader, I don't feel alone in my Business, I have a Team with me for the good and bad – that is priceless.

Thanks Lucy, I love working with you!"

Claire Humphreys – Pink Aubergine Branded Bakes

"Working with Lucy has been an invaluable experience. As my sister and I step up and take more ownership in the family business, Lucy has been helping us gain the necessary skills and insight to running the business. You can really feel her wealth of knowledge, and her passion and excitement is infectious!

We always feel so empowered and ready to take on the world after a session with Lucy."

Elle Moran – JCM Business Solutions

"I first came across Lucy during the height of the pandemic where she amazingly gave her time and expertise for free to help business owners navigate the unprecedented situation. As a result, we reached out to Lucy to support us with our Brand marketing strategy and ensure our mission and brand values were clear so that future activities are in line and not just a sporadic mess!

What Lucy is sure to tease out are the core drivers behind the marketing strategy and the commercial angle to ensure a return on the investment. For me there is nothing more amazing that seeing marketing deliver tangible, profit generating results. We have only scratched the surface and know with Lucy's support we will become the leading company in our sector."

Lisa Kettell – Kettell Windows

"If you're thinking of working with Lucy, she is so passionate about supporting you and your business and will be your biggest cheerleader. She'll pull out your stories, help you see your strengths and make you realise that anything is possible."

Rachel Spencer – Publicity for Pet Businesses

"The help I've received is vast. I've gained confidence to put my ceramics business out there, taken control of my social media and have gained invaluable insights into communications. Running an independent business is challenging, so having the support from Lucy has been really helpful on practical and emotional levels. I would never have had the confidence to do a live gift experience, live videos or apply to have my pottery at a month-long exhibition. Lucy is great to work with, full of amazing advice and just such a lovely person to spend time with. She is personal, professional, and passionate."

Lynne Taylor – Organic Ceramics

"Having Lucy as part of your world is what everybody needs! Having her guidance and support has been crucial to the development of my business and myself. The mastermind she has created means that you are not alone with the challenges that running a small business brings and she has given us a safe space for sharing the frustrations as well as celebrating the joy. I can't imagine not having Lucy as part of my life!"

Sara Woolrich – JCM Business Solutions

"I LOVE working with Lucy. You listen so well to what each of your clients' needs (and that can be so different) and then you meet them where they are. You take away some of their pressures of being self-employed and are so generous in what you offer. Thank you."

Claire Bradshaw – Claire Bradshaw Associates

"It was the best days learning I have had for years. I feel motivated and want to get started."

Rob Booth – LGS Consultancy

"I love the community of like-minded business women you've created who support each other to thrive together in a way that feels ethical and full of integrity."

Helen Harding – Coach-Mentor for Holistic Practitioners

Lucy's has really helped me to focus in on my objectives and given me not only excellent one to one support to help me achieve them, but also the support and friendship of other business owners – this has been invaluable during such a difficult year. Thanks to the Mastermind programme I'm feeling more confident and positive than I ever thought I would as we come out of a year of lockdowns. Thank you so much Lucy and rest of the Mastermind Group!"

Suzanne Horton – Puddle Ducks Greater Manchester, Worcestershire and Derbyshire

REFERENCES

1. Future-Proof your Business

1. Source: Longman dictionary

3. An Inside Out Approach to your brand

1. Source: Oxford languages
2. Source: 'True Gen': Generation Z and its implications for companies
3. Source: 'True Gen': Generation Z and its implications for companies

9. Becoming the brand that does

1. *Source:* *https://www.forbes.com/sites/henrydevries/2018/08/29/geoff-ramm-on-treating-customers-like-beyonce-george-clooney-or-brad-pitt/?sh=20b79ada7d27*
2. Source: Hubspot.

11. Word of mouth

1. Source: Bureau of Labor Statistics, as reported by Fundera
2. *Source: https://www.theguardian.com/technology/2008/aug/03/internet.email*
3. *Source:* *https://www.nytimes.com/2013/02/19/science/the-average-american-knows-how-many-people.html*

13. The TripAdvisor effect

1. Source: Nielson
2. *Source : (Nielson)*
3. *Source: Nielson*

ABOUT THE AUTHOR

Nicola Wardle Photography

Lucy Rennie is a communications and marketing expert, business strategist and mentor with over 25 years' experience working in international business. In her most recent role, Lucy spent ten years in France and Luxembourg as Head of Communications within the global steel and mining company, ArcelorMittal supporting more than 300 sites worldwide before launching her own business in 2015. She still has her own hard hat and steel cap shoes. She speaks fluent French, and bien sûr has a real love of French wine, cheese and baguettes!

Today, Lucy works with large and small corporate organisations, advising, coaching and mentoring business owners, managers and their teams to develop strategies for consistent growth, build trust and attract more of the right kind of people and clients to their business.

A huge champion for small business, and a massive believer in the fact that people do business with people, Lucy Rennie is on a mission to share her love for small business and to help you to harness the power of people, relationships and goodwill and reap the benefits of what she refers to as the "TripAdvisor effect.

Lucy lives and works on the side of a big hill overlooking Whaley Bridge, a beautiful village on the edge of the Peak District with her husband Paul, daughter Ellia, stepson Josh and crazy chocolate Labrador, Kylo Ren.

A massive Star Wars fan, Lucy loves to spend her time running, cooking, reading, and listening to books and podcasts about business.

Get in touch

If you have enjoyed this journey with me, I would love to hear your thoughts and takeaways. You can get in touch with me at lucy@lrcomms.co.uk or why not come and join me in my FREE Facebook community, *Communicate with Purpose*? A free group for small business owners looking to grow, develop and future-proof their business in a way that works and feels good for them.

Have a listen to my new *Future-Proof Your Business podcast*.

Visit my website: www.iamlucyrennie.com

instagram.com/IamLucyRennie
linkedin.com/in/lucyrennie1

Printed in Great Britain
by Amazon

16366289R00113